Editor

Warships fascinate people for a number of reasons. Battleships were in their day the most complex pieces of moving machinery on earth, and the aircraft carrier and Polaris submarine can make similar claims today for they make use of the most advanced technology known to Man. But warships also fought in campaigns of all kinds, from great fleet battles down to skirmishes involving small ships, and they were manned and built by generations of highly skilled men.

The naval historian, the ship enthusiast and the modeller all have a vested interest in accurate sources of information about warships, their weapons and their operations. Even the social historian and the uniform collector need to know about the ships in which officers and ratings served. *Warship* meets these diverse needs by providing a quarterly journal devoted to warships and their history.

This first issue contains features which reflect the editorial policy; the well-known American modeller Lawrence Sowinski writes about his model of the World War II light cruiser *Wilkes-Barre,* John Campbell describes the origins of the British 48000-ton 'G3' class battlecruisers of 1921-22, Alan Raven covers the changes in appearance of British destroyers in World War II, and David Lyon deals with the four-funnelled 'Town' class cruisers of World War I. Conway Maritime Press is fortunate in having a vast picture library, and so a permanent feature of *Warship* will be photographs of old and new warships. To give some idea of the range and variety of the collection, the first issue contains a sample of nineteenth and twentieth century warships, but future issues will contain series devoted to single ships, or an opera-

tion, for example. We also want to emphasise quality of illustrations as much as quantity, with large photographs to show all possible details. All photographs belonging to the Conway Picture Library can be supplied as prints.

One important virtue of a quarterly journal is that feature articles can be of greater length. It is not our policy to limit features to a length which fits a single issue, but rather to spread them over three or four parts. This, we hope, will enable our contributors to do justice to their subjects and makes each issue more varied.

There is no limit on subjects. We welcome contributions on weapons, shipbuilding, operations or any other aspect of warships and the job that they do. Obviously we will concentrate on nineteenth and twentieth century warships initially, but we will also look back at eighteenth century warships from time to time, because in many ways the basic problems of ship-design have not changed in 200 years. For the modeller we will provide articles about sources for photographs and plans, and for the book-collector we will review books. In one respect we will be slightly unorthodox; we intend to have retrospective reviews of some books and plans which have been in print for some years, if they are of value to our readers.

Having stated our policy we now look to the readers for confirmation and guidance. Advice and criticism will be welcomed, as our intention remains to offer correct and factual information for everybody who shares our interest in warships.

The Editor

2

This is the first of four parts, comprising a detailed description of the British capital ships which were designed between the end of the First World War and the signing of the Washington Treaty. The author is a metallurgist by training, and apart from being the author of a Warship Monograph on the *Queen Elizabeth* class battleships he has written an unpublished account of Jutland. The later instalments of the article will include sketch designs for the various projects which preceded the 'G3s' similar to that of HMS *Hood*.

Detail from a painting by Geoff Hunt, showing two of the late 1920 designs as they might have appeared. The battleship (foreground), design 'M3', would have carried 9–18inch guns at 23 knots. In the background appears battlecruiser design 'H3b', also featuring 18inch guns. Both designs will be described in a later issue of *Warship*.

Washington's Cherrytrees

THE EVOLUTION OF THE BRITISH 1921-22 CAPITAL SHIPS

By N J M CAMPBELL

The four ships known as the *G3s,* or more usually but inaccurately as the 'Super-*Hoods',* cancelled under the Washington Naval Treaty of 1922, were the largest and in many ways the most powerful battleships or battlecruisers ever ordered for the British Navy. In spite of this no adequate description of these ships has even been published as the account in Oscar Parkes' *British Battleships* is incomplete, and the plan and elevation given are not those of the final design. The origins of these ships lie in the very inferior position as regards battleships and battlecruisers, in which the British Navy was likely to be in the 1920s, compared with the United States and in all probability Japan. In November 1918 there were thirty-three 'dread-nought' battleships and nine battle-cruisers in the British Navy, sixteen and none respectively in the American, and five and four in the Japanese. Under construction were the four battlecruisers of the *Hood* class, of which one had been launched, as against four American battleships (one launched and nearly complete) and two Japanese battle-ships. None of the British ships had heavier guns than 15 inch, while one of the American ships under con-struction, the *Maryland,* and both Japanese, the *Nagato* and *Mutsu* would have 16 inch. There was a large margin of British superiority here, even allowing for the obsoles-cent features of many of the older British ships, but by the end of 1920 the position had drastically changed. The *Hood* had been completed, but her three sisterships had been can-celled, one battleship, the *Canada,* taken over for the war, had been returned to Chile, and four battle-ships and two battlecruisers, all with 12 inch guns, had been stricken from the lists. No new ships were under construction, and of the twenty-eight battleships and eight battlecruisers remaining, six and two respectively, armed with 12 inch guns were likely to be of subsidiary use only.

Meanwhile the United States had completed two of their four new ships, the other two would complete in 1921 and a further very large new programme was in hand. This included three sister ships of the *Maryland,* all three to be launched in 1921, six much larger battleships of the *South Dakota* class, of which five had been laid down in 1920 and the sixth to follow in the spring of 1921, and six large and very fast battlecruisers of the *Lexington* class, of which four had been laid down in 1920, and the remaining two would be begun in January and June 1921. Progress in Japan was less well-known in London than that in the United States, but the *Nagato* was completed, the *Mutsu* was launched and would complete in 1921, two more battleships, the *Kaga* and *Tosa,* and two battlecruisers, the *Amagi* and *Akagi* had been laid down, and further ships would follow.

It is true that, like the British 12 inch ships, six of the older Ameri-can battleships, as well as one of the Japanese, could be classed as only of subsidiary use, but this did not alter the inferiority of the best of the existing British ships to those laid down in the United States in 1920. The six *South Dakotas* were to be of 43 200 tons normal displacement with 12 x 16 inch/50 cal guns, and the six *Lexingtons* of 43 500 tons with 8 x 16 inch/50 cal guns, while the lone *Hood* of an actual 43 670 tons, though better protected than the *Lexingtons,* had only 8 x 15 inch/ 42 cal guns. None of the British battleships mounted more than 8 x 15 inch/42 cal, and the actual normal displacement of the largest did not exceed 31 000 tons.

To correct this situation it was originally intended to order three new battleships and one new battle-cruiser early in the financial year of 1921-22, and the same numbers again late in the financial year of 1922-23, this being the maximum that could be conveniently built without fresh heavy capital equipment. This was subsequently modified to four battlecruisers in the middle of 1921-22, and if the Washington Treaty had not been negotiated, it is to be presumed that four battleships would have followed in 1922-23. The reasons for giving priority to the battlecruisers do not appear to be on record, but seven of the eight existing British ships of this type were very poorly protected and quite unfit to oppose 14 inch, let alone 16 inch guns. Also the very high speed of the

Nelson and *Rodney* carried the 16inch Mk I ordered in 1921.

CPL. W/1/014

Lexingtons, 33¼ knots, seems to have made a great impression. It was intended to mount 18 inch guns in the new battleships, and of the ordnance factories in Britain, only Elswick could handle this size in production without difficulty on existing plant, whereas 16 inch guns could be ordered from other firms.

Much interesting design and experimental work was put in hand in the period between the end of the First World War and the ordering of the *G3s,* and to understand how the *G3* design came to incorporate so many new features, an account must be given of this work.

Considering first the items which were necessary to a large warship, the development of a new heavy gun was one of the most important. The latest 'standard' British heavy gun in 1918 was the 15 inch Mark I of 42 calibres bore-length and weighing 100 tons with breech mechanism. It fired a 1920lb projectile with a new gun muzzle velocity of 2472 ft per second (fs) and was exceptionally accurate. It was however quite outclassed by the American 16 inch/50 cal gun of 137 tons which fired a 2100lb projectile at 2750fs while the 16 inch/45 cal of 105 tons in the *Maryland* class had a muzzle velocity of 2600fs with the same shell as the 16 inch/50 cal. However during the First World War, three 18 inch/40 cal guns had been made by Elswick to Woolwich drawings, but though various capital ship sketch designs had been prepared on the basis of this gun, the only ships which actually carried it were (most unsuitably) the *Furious* in her hybrid aricraft carrier/cruiser period, and with more reason

the monitors *General Wolfe* and *Lord Clive.*

In point of fact this was a very good gun resembling an enlarged 15 inch Mark I, and weighing 149 tons, although it was too short and its ballistics were spoilt by the inability to produce a larger-grain propellant than the usual MD45 in wartime. Thus the muzzle velocity was limited to barely 2275fs with a 3320lb shell, though satisfactory results were obtained with super-charges which gave about 2400fs. It was clear that something better was needed for new capital ships, and in November 1919 the Director of Naval Ordnance asked the Ordnance Committee to obtain designs for 18 inch/45 cal guns.

It was decided to compare a gun of the usual wire-wound construction with one in which the wire did not extend for more than about half the length, and also with one built without wire, described as of 'all-steel' construction. Numerous designs for all three were prepared by Vickers, Elswick and Woolwich, and after mid-1920 were always referred to as '16 inch/50 cal', though this probably deceived no one. Eventually orders were placed on 22 December 1920 for a 'half-wire' gun with Vickers and for an 'all-steel' one with Elswick, and on 20 January 1921 for a wire-wound gun with Woolwich. A fourth gun built on the then Krupp principles as far as they could be adapted to a bag-loading gun, using this firm's normal construction method of precision shrinking of relatively short steel tubes, remained a project only.

It was thought that production guns would be fully wire-wound as the necessary tests on the others

would not be completed in time. The Woolwich design was for a relatively light gun, of 134.5 tons including breech mechanism, and with a 3320lb shell the new gun muzzle velocity was expected to be around 2500fs. As explained below the shell weight was reduced to 2916lb so that the likely muzzle velocity would be in the region of 2650fs. The difficulties of making MD cordite of a sufficiently large grain were to be overcome by using an 'oval' section – actually a square with semi-circles on a pair of opposite sides – until such time as the 'solventless' cordite developed at Ardeer had passed its lengthy tests for acceptance as a service propellant. The three guns were never completed and were cancelled on 30 January 1922.

The Admiralty requested Sir Robert Hadfield of the famous steel firm to stop talking about 20 inch and 21 inch APC shells in 1920, but this was apparently done to prevent other countries thinking that guns of these calibres might be adopted, and there does not seem to have been any intention of so doing, though Elswick could have handled a 20 inch of about 42 calibres on their existing plant. The Japanese built a 19 inch gun which split in testing, and a second one that was still in existence in December 1945, while the United States constructed an 18 inch/48 cal: a ponderous weapon of nearly 178 tons, firing a 2900lb shell at 2700fs. It was later linered down to a 16 inch/57 cal and then back to an 18 inch. No other naval guns of 18 inch or over appear to have been built at this time, although the French began design work on a 17.7 inch (45cm)

Gun	Nationality	Bore length (calibres)	Weight (tons)	Weight of projectile (pounds)	Muzzle velocity (feet per second)
15in Mk I (in general service)	British	42	100	1920	2472
16in	US	50	137	2100	2750
16in (Maryland class)	US	45	105	2100	2600
16in Mk I (Nelson, Rodney)	British	45	108	2048	2575
17.7in	French	45	126	2950	2750
18in	US	48	178	2900	2700
18in (Furious)	British	40	149	3320	2275
18in (Woolwich design)	British	45	134.5	2916	2650
19in	Japanese	—	—	—	—

in 1920.

It was realised that although 18 inch guns were suitable for battleships of under 50 000 tons, the same was very doubtful for battlecruisers. Consideration was given to 15 inch/50 cal and to 16.5 inch/45 cal and 50 cal guns, but in January 1921 it was decided to use 16 inch/45 cal.

A normal wire-wound design was prepared by Woolwich and the first guns were ordered from Elswick on 22 August 1921. These guns, the 16 inch Mark I, later mounted in *Nelson* and *Rodney*, weighed 108 tons and were intended to have a muzzle velocity of 2700fs with a 2048lb shell. Trials gave 2670fs but wear was rapid as was loss of accuracy, stripping of the rifling occurring from the 'hammer' action of the short-bodied, long-headed projectile. The new gun muzzle velocity was reduced to 2575fs the gun thereby becoming exceptionally accurate, and by 1938 modified rifling was being introduced on relining, which gave at least 25fs more muzzle velocity.

It may be noted that to hasten the test programme one of the Army's 18 inch howitzers and one of the 18 inch/40 cal guns that had been set aside for the test programme for the 18 inch/45 cal, were linered down to

16 inch. The gun (that originally in *Furious*) was eventually scrapped in 1947 and the howitzer in 1951. The other two 18 inch/40 cal guns were sold for scrap in July 1933, and the persistent story that they went to Singapore is quite unfounded.

The three major troubles of British ships' armament in the First World War, ineffective armour-piercing shell, unsafe magazine and ammunition supply arrangements and unstable propellant, had been largely overcome by the end of 1918. Doubts still existed on the performance of the longer AP shells, 15 inch and 1400lb 13.5 inch, at oblique impact and it was felt that a shell of reduced weight/(diameter)^3 ratio might well be better, in spite of the greater loss of striking energy from air resistance. This opinion, which may have originated in the light 1653lb shell favoured by the Germans for their 15 inch seemed to be confirmed by the indifferent performance of some 15 inch 1920lb shells, and by 1250lb 13.5 inch behaving better than some 1400lb. As a result the new 18 inch shell was fixed at 2916lb in December 1920 and the 16 inch at 2048lb in June 1921, instead of at 3320 and 2330lb which corresponded with the 1920lb 15 inch. Later tests in 1922-3 with

15 inch shells of improved quality showed that the heavier ones behaved just as well as the lighter, but the 18 inch had by then been cancelled, and the 16 inch projectiles were not altered, though for the 16 inch guns to have been mounted in the *Lion* class of 1939, a shell of 2375lb was adopted, and the United States went to 2700lb for the 16 inch guns of their more modern battleships in the Second World War.

On propellant safety, attempts were made to find a more protective covering than a single silk bag without going to metal QF cases, but these had little success. It is noteworthy that no trials involving several tons of propellant, as ignited in the *Seydlitz* at the Dogger Bank battle in 1915, were ever carried out, and that trials to investigate the results of igniting a charge in a QF magazine, were not approved until November 1939 and were then cancelled in August 1940. One discovery of major importance was that the venting magazine cases, used to prevent a spontaneously igniting charge exploding violently, were neither flash- non water-tight and non-venting cases were introduced in 1923, the risk of a further ship blowing up from decomposing propellant being considered accept-

8

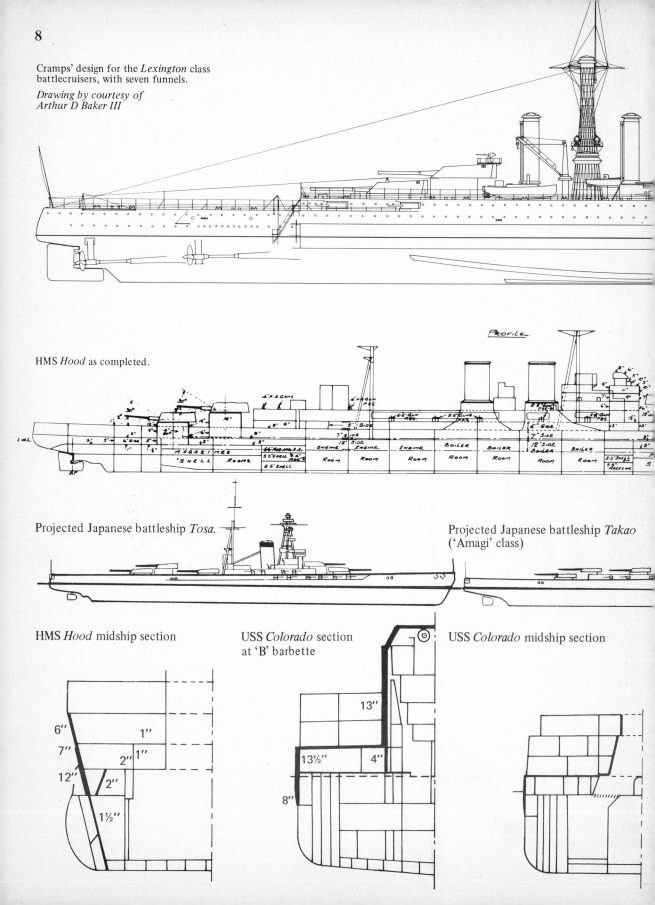

Cramps' design for the *Lexington* class battlecruisers, with seven funnels.

Drawing by courtesy of Arthur D Baker III

HMS *Hood* as completed.

Projected Japanese battleship *Tosa*.

Projected Japanese battleship *Takao* ('Amagi' class)

HMS *Hood* midship section

USS *Colorado* section at 'B' barbette

USS *Colorado* midship section

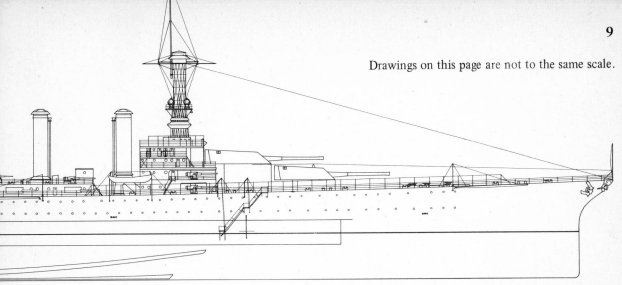

Drawings on this page are not to the same scale.

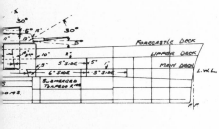

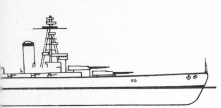

able with greatly improved standards of propellant manufacture. This discovery seems to have been originally made in 1920 when 12 inch and 4 inch magazine cases, loaded in the *New Zealand* on a cold and rainy February day, were subsequently found to have admitted moisture.

Triple gun mountings had been considered for 12 inch guns when the *St Vincent* class were being designed in 1906-7, but they had never been used in the British Navy up to 1918 except for the 4 inch secondary armament in the *Renown* and *Courageous* classes. Triple 12 inch mountings, mainly if not entirely designed by British firms, had been used in the Italian and Russian navies, while the Austrians had also introduced 12 inch and the United States 14 inch triple mountings. Owing to the shorter length that had to be protected by heavy armour, the use of three triple turrets, two forward and one aft, instead of four twins, saved about 1000 tons in a 50 000 ton ship and gained a gun, so that the advantages were appreciable. In 1921 trials were carried out with a makeshift 15 inch triple mounting — not a triple turret — in the *Lord Clive,* and showed that no unacceptable loss of accuracy was likely to occur if the three guns were fired together. The use of a triple 12 inch turret from the Russian battleship *Volya,* formerly the *Imperator Alexander III,* which was in British hands for a time, had been previously suggested but this fell through.

Meanwhile triple and twin turret designs from Elswick and Vickers for calibres from 18 inch down to 15 inch

had been considered, and it was decided to adopt Elswick 18 inch and 16 inch triple designs. Unfortunately no complete drawings of the 18 inch triple which was the first in point of time, appear to have survived, but it would seem to have resembled the 16 inch except that power handling of the charges in the magazine would have been used. The mean roller path diameter was 37ft 6in, the mean barbette diameter 40ft 4in, distance between gun axes 8ft 6in, and the revolving weight 1700–1730 tons, which appears to be on the light side. The 16 inch turret was similar to that afterwards mounted in *Nelson* and *Rodney* but it would have had a heavier shield and also auxiliary loading, with mean barbette and roller path diameters of 38ft 6in and 33ft, and revolving weight estimated as 1560 (later 1514) tons, compared with 1464–1483 tons in the *Nelson* class. Considerable changes were made in these mountings from previous British practice, as the cartridge and pusher shell hoists were not broken at the working chamber. A maximum elevation of 45° is often mentioned but it is unlikely that more than 40° would have been provided, with loading at about 3° elevation.

In torpedoes the most important development was the British work on oxygen-enriched air, which led to the 24.5 inch Mark I torpedo first run at Loch Long in April 1924. This had a range of 15 000 yards at 35 kts, or 20 000 at 30 with a 750lb explosive charge and could have had one of 1000lb. The most powerful torpedo used in the First World War, the German 23.6 inch H8, had a 540lb explosive charge and ranges of about 15 000 yards at 28 kts, or 18 000 at 25½. The oxygen enriched 21 inch Mark VII was developed for the 8 inch gunned cruisers, but there was general nervousness over the oxygen equipment, known for reasons of secrecy as 'No 1 Air Compressor Room', and interest faded on the introduction of the highly efficient Brotherhood Burner Cycle engine with un-enriched air, so that it was left to the Japanese to demonstrate the potentialities of oxygen torpedoes in the Second World War.

On armour protection it was shown that even 10 inch vertical plates were of little value against efficient 15 inch APC shells, and that a barbette for example, was far better protected by 14 inch armour in one thickness than by a 7 inch upper belt plus 7 inch on the barbette. All credit is due to the American designers of the *Nevada* and *Oklahoma,* (laid down in 1912) for realising this, and doing away with side armour above the main deck so that this deck, the principal belt and the barbettes could be thickened. Important trials were carried out in 1921 on the *Baden,* the last German battleship to be completed in the First World War, which had been beached and salved at Scapa Flow. The trials cannot be described in detail here, but a total of thirty-one 15 inch shells of various types were fired by the monitors *Terror* and *Erebus,* the striking velocity being 1550 or 1380fs equivalent to 15 500 and 21 800 yards with 4-calibre radius head shells. At 1550fs a 14 inch turret face plate was pierced by an APC shell at 18½° to the normal, though the shell was blind, but at 30° to the normal the 14 inch conning tower resisted an APC shell fairly well. An indication of the improvement in APC shells is given by the fact that it took ten attempts with a total of 106 15oz wet gun-cotton slabs before the above blind shell was destroyed, whereas pre-1914 a single attempt with four such slabs usually sufficed. Another APC shell at 1550fs pierced the 10 inch upper belt at 14½° to the normal and burst 38ft from impact against the funnel casings after going through the 1.2 inch longitudinal splinter bulkhead and the ½ inch main deck. The armour gratings were unshipped and two boilers were disabled.

Of the several shells that pierced 6¾ inch armour, the most remarkable was a semi-armour-piercing (SAPC) at 1380fs which pierced the battery armour and then broke up on 'B' barbette (also 6¾ inch) which was struck at 42° to the normal. A piece of armour 4ft x 3ft was punched out, and the turret would have been jammed and put out of action. It is safe to say that this shell would have had little effect striking a 13½ inch barbette directly. Of other information obtained in the trials, the most important item was perhaps that turret roof girders and supports should be greatly increased in strength.

The *Baden* was then used for trials with bombs detonated at rest on the weather deck or upper works. A total of five bombs, one 1800lb, one 550lb heavy case, three 520lb light case, were employed, and superficial damage was done; only the 550lb holed the deck below that on which the bomb was placed. A 520lb bomb was also detonated on the 4 inch roof of 'Y' turret with little effect. No likely armour-piercing bomb at that time would have equalled a steeply falling heavy shell in piercing a thick deck, but it would seem that the 550lb bomb might well have been detonated below the 1.2 inch forecastle deck instead of on the boat deck.

Much larger-scale bomb trials were carried out in 1921 by the United States on the ex-German *Ostfriesland,* one of the older dreadnought battleships. According to British information thirty-three 250lb and 300lb and nineteen 550lb and 600lb bombs were first dropped with thirteen direct hits of which three were blind. Three 550lb bombs exploded in the water near the hull. Examination showed that the hull was undamaged

and the protective deck which had a minimum thickness of 1.6 inches was not pierced. Certain compartments, however, flooded during the night. Next day five 1000lb bombs were dropped with three direct hits which would not have placed the ship out of action, and then six 2000lb bombs of which two were direct hits and two burst in succession underwater close to the hull, sinking the ship in 14 minutes. It had been intended to examine the ship after each bomb that caused damage so that useful information could be obtained, but the notorious Brigadier-General William Mitchell who was in charge of the aircraft side of the trials, pre-ferred a propaganda success for air power. The undoubtedly very power-ful mining effect of heavy bombs was thus not properly investigated until the British trials on the *Monarch* in 1923, noted on a later page. The *Ostfriesland's* underwater protection consisted of a 1.2 inch-1 inch torpedo bulkhead at a maximum of 14¾ft inboard, the space between the shell plating and the torpedo bulk-head being divided approximately in half by a thin longitudinal bulkhead. The outboard half consisted of empty compartments and the inner was occupied by the protective coal bunkers. This system was used in later First World War German battle-ships such as the *Baden,* but with detail improvements and an increase in the torpedo bulkhead to 2 inches. The reports seen by the writer do not mention the condition of the bunker doors in the *Ostfriesland's* torpedo bulkhead or the coal content of the protective bunkers at the time of the trial, which would have been matters of much importance.

The underwater protection of British ships from 1914 was developed by model experiments and full-scale trials on structures built into the 'Chatham Float', but the test pro-gramme was often behind design and then served to confirm rather than initiate. The original external bulges, the value of which had been well proved in the First World War, were largely incorporated in the hull struc-ture in the *Hood*. In this ship the torpedo bulkhead was 1½ inches and the maximum 'bulge' width outboard of this about 10½ft. The outer part

of the 'bulge' consisted of empty water-tight compartments and the inner contained five rows of steel crushing tubes. Where space permit-ted there was an additional ¾ inch bulkhead inboard of the 1½ inch one, and the space between was mostly occupied by fuel oil. This system was designed to withstand a 500lb TNT charge in contact, and tests on the Chatham Float in 1919-20 showed that equally good protection and a saving in weight were obtained if the crushing tube compartments were filled with water instead of tubes. Sufficient knowledge was considered to be available to design a system for the new ships to withstand 750lb TNT in contact.

The possibility of a magazine ex-ploding from a mine detonating below it, was given much attention, and it had been found better to place the magazines below the shell rooms, reversing the previous British practice, so that water would enter the maga-zine at once and prevent any serious fire. In the new ships the double bottom was to be 7ft deep to try to improve protection, and in July 1921 a 350lb mine was detonated under the Chatham Float which had been fitted to represent a 16 inch shell room and magazine of the *G3s*. There was no sign whatever of a propellant fire, and results were otherwise fairly satisfactory, but much later tests showed that the 7ft double bottom was undesirable as its stiffness tended to damage the bases of transverse bulkheads over a wider area than did a shallower structure. No tests seem to have been carried out with the 1918 British magnetic ground mine, known as 'Sinker IM' which had a 1000lb TNT charge.

An important matter which needed improvement in British ships was the capacity of the pumps, as those in the *Baden* could dispose of 8100 tons per hour outside the main machinery compartments, as against only 4450 tons in the *Hood* which was of nearly 50 per cent greater displacement.

There is no doubt that the Board of Admiralty acted correctly in can-celling the three further ships of the *Hood* type on 27 February 1919. The original design for the class had been submitted on 27 March 1916, and

legend displacement was at that time 36 300 tons. Since then protection had been much increased so that the *Hood's* legend displacement was 41 200 tons and actually 42 670 as hull and machinery were well over weight. Further alterations were approved in August 1918 for the other three ships involving a better distribu-tion of protection at the price of a total of 120 fewer rounds of 15 inch, and a very slight loss in speed, but it was better to start afresh which was the easier to approve as none of the three were far advanced.

It must be noted that it was not the weight devoted to protection which was at fault in the *Hood* as this amounted to 13 650 tons out of 42 670, a higher proportion than in the *G3s* which had 14 440 out of 48 400 tons, but the amount wasted on medium and thin armour. Also the *Hood's* metacentric height was undesirably low at 3.3ft, and as noted previously, the 15 inch/42 cal gun was no longer adequate.
(To be continued)

The ex-German battleship *Baden* listing after firing trials in 1920-21. Note that 'A' turret has been removed, presumably for examination of its machinery, while 'B' and 'X' turrets are trained on the beam to allow firing against the face plates.

CPL. W/1/002

model Shipwright

A Quarterly Journal of Ships and Ship Models

Editors John L Bowen, C Eng, MRINA
Robert Gardiner
Art Editor Ray Fishwick
Consultant Editor Arthur L Tucker

Model Shipwright is a quarterly journal devoted to all aspects of scale ship modelling, from the research stage to the final display, sailing or even photography of the completed vessel. The articles are contributed by practical ship modellers from all over the world, whose knowledge, experience and expertise are an inspiration to beginner and expert alike. All features are illustrated with plans, drawings and photographs, so that the volumes of 'Model Shipwright' will build up into a work of permanent reference, to be consulted time and time again by the discerning modelmaker.

In the coming year there will be a number of articles of particular interest to warship modellers, both on the construction and the research sides. These include:

- A series by Lawrence Sowinski on his superb collection of warship miniatures.
- Ships boats in the era of sail, by Jack Kitzerow.
- The American Revolutionary War privateer 'Oliver Cromwell', a serialised feature in which Harold Hahn, one of America's finest modellers describes the career of the original vessels and his fine model.
- An article from Russia, complete with plans, on the cruiser 'Ochakov' and the Black Sea Fleet mutiny of 1905.
- A major new series of gun mounting drawings, prepared and described by John Roberts.
- Modelling the 'Popoffkas' by Colin Gross.
- A detailed description of a 6-foot model in tinplate of 'Pheasant', one of the famous 'Black Swans' of the World War II support groups.

There is also a complete review section devoted to the latest in books, plans, tools, materials and kits.

Technical Data

Page size	8 1/2'' x 7 3/8''
Number of pages	100
Plans and diagrams (average)	60
Photographs (average)	65
Binding	Semi-stiff

Published by Conway Maritime Press Ltd, in September, December, March and June of each year. A quarterly part contains not less than 100 pages and is bound in durable, semi-stiff covers for long shelf-life.

Subscription Rates

Payment in the UK and Ireland may be made by cheque or postal order; overseas payments by International Money Order or by personal cheques in the above currencies, which include packing and surface mail. All cheques and postal orders to be crossed and made payable to Conway Maritime Press Ltd, and endorsed 'A/C Payee'.

Australia	$10.50	New Zealand	$10.50
Canada	$16.00	USA	$18.00
France	Fr 75.00	United Kingdom	£7.00
Germany	DM38.00	(includes £1.00 postage in UK and Ireland)	

Orders

To obtain your subscription, please send the following information:

Name and address to which copies should be sent, in block capitals.

The issue on which you would like your subscription to commence: September 1976, issue 17; December 1976, issue 18; March 1977, issue 19; June 1977, issue 20. You will receive four issues followed by a reminder that your subscription needs renewing.

Please state if you are renewing an existing subscription.

Enclose your order with the remittance and send to **The Subscription Manager, Model Shipwright, 2 Nelson Road, London SE10, UK.**

Back issues. Limited numbers of many issues are still available. Details from the publishers.

Bridge detail of HMS *Pheasant*, a 1/4'' = 1'0'' scale model in tinplate.

British Destroyer Appearance

IN WORLD WAR II

PART 1
FLEET
DESTROYERS
1939-42

By ALAN RAVEN

Alan Raven is a modeller, but about six years ago he decided to produce modellers' plans of British warships. He has also produced several of the Ensign series: *King George V,* 'Flower' class (with Antony Preston), *Queen Elizabeth* and *Southampton* classes (with John Roberts). He and John Roberts have also recently completed a large and detailed study of British battleships.

HMS *Jupiter*, one of the handsome 'J' or *Javelin* class destroyers in late 1940 or early 1941, with only five torpedo tubes. She has quadruple .5inch machine guns as close-range AA defence and no radar is fitted

Partridge, one of the early War Emergency Programme destroyers, late in 1941. She has been fitted with gunnery and air-warning radar.

From the start of hostilities in September 1939 until about April of the following year, all the destroyers in service during this period retained either their original or pre-war appearance. The most distinctive aspect of this appearance was the fairly complicated lofty rig which comprised not only the normal foremast arrangement but also a mainmast, either a pole, or a tripod type that was almost the same height. The fitting of a mainmast to carry the main W/T aerials from the foremast meant a large number of aerial wires strung over a considerable area of the deck.

The Norwegian Campaign and the subsequent scale of air attack against surface warships including destroyers, not only demonstrated the inadequacies of the existing close range AA capabilities but also the need for greater sky arcs for the weapons already carried. These sky arcs were greatly restricted by the complicated rig, the chief cause of which was the fitting of the mainmast. Thus destroyers under repair or refit from around April 1940 had their mainmast removed, with the W/T aerials taken to a small aerial spreader attached to the after control position. Not only did this measure improve the sky arcs but it also enabled a single 4 inch AA gun to be fitted in place of the after bank of torpedo tubes. As well as ships under refit or

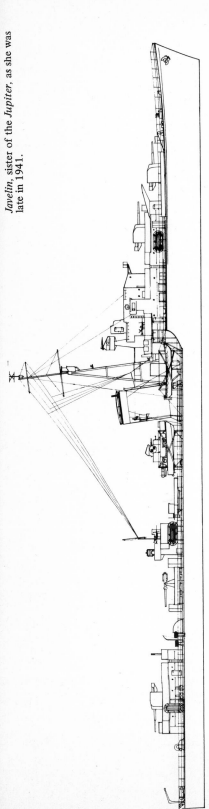

The Type I 'Hunt' class *Holderness* early in 1942. She has gunnery and search radar and carries a 2pdr bow-chaser and 20mm AA guns.

repair, the new ships completing, (in the case of destroyers, the Type I *Hunts*) also incorporated these features. The drawings of *Jupiter* and *Garth* as they appeared during mid-1940 accurately reflect these early war features.

During the autumn of 1940 the first radar sets for destroyers and other small ships became available. This first radar set, known as Type 286, required an aerial array that consisted of six 'yagi' antennae, that had to be supported by a fairly large and complex framework. As this set was used for surface warning, and did not operate in the microwave band, to obtain any sort of worthwhile results on surface contacts the aerial array had to be positioned at the highest possible point, and in the larger type of fleet destroyers enough reserve of top-weight was available to allow the fitting of the aerial at the head of the foremast. This can be seen in the drawings of *Ashanti* and *Holderness*.

The year 1941 saw the completion of many units of the L and M class destroyers. As one would expect, these important new ships were fitted out wherever possible with the most up-to-date equipment; this included the newly available single 20mm hand-worked Oerlikon gun. In ships of the L and M class this meant at least two mountings, as shown in the drawings of *Lance*, or four as in the drawing of *Laforey*. Where new des-

troyers carried only two 20mm
mountings, these were almost always
positioned in sponsons attached to
each side of the after control position.
As shown on *Laforey* and *Lance* the
AA weapon in the bridge wings is the
quadruple 0.5 inch machine gun, and
this mounting was extremely common
in this position during 1941/42. In
some units of the *O* and *P* class completing in 1941 and early 1942 two
twin power-mounted 0.5 inch
machine guns were carried either in
the bridge wings, for example *Onslow*,
or on either side of the after control
position. In some units of the *Tribal*
class (period 1941), for example *Zulu*,
two single 20mm on the after deckhouse, two quadruple 0.5 inch MGs
amidships, and two single hand-
worked 2 pounder pom-poms in the
bridge wings were carried. The combination of 20mm and 0.5 inch MGs
on fleet destroyers during 1941 and
early 1942 was very common.

As well as the fitting of the
Oerlikon mounting, new and improved radar sets began to be fitted; these
were Types 290 and 291, for air and
surface warning, replacing Type 286,
and for gunnery purposes, Type 285.

The aerial arrays for Types 290
and 291 were identical and also quite
small; the reduction in weight over
Type 286 meant that in every case
the aerial could be carried at the foremast head. The actual equipment for
the radar had to be housed some-

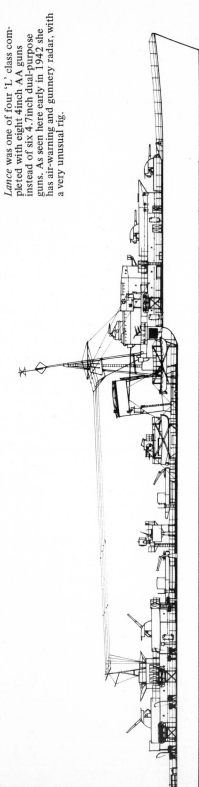

Lance was one of four 'L' class completed with eight 4inch AA guns
instead of six 4.7inch dual-purpose
guns. As seen here early in 1942 she
has air-warning and gunnery radar, with
a very unusual rig.

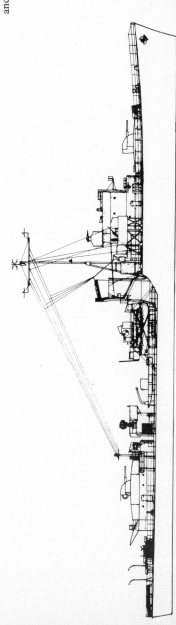

The Type III 'Hunt' *Wensleydale* in
1942, showing the distinctive appearance of this group.

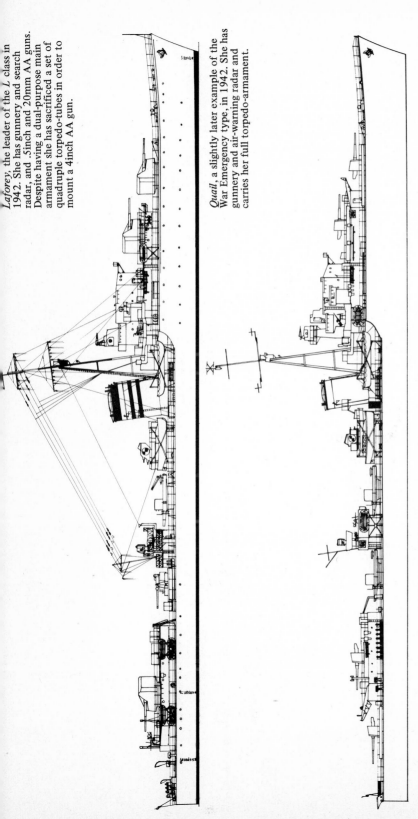

Laforey, the leader of the *L* class in 1942. She has gunnery and search radar, and .5inch and 20mm AA guns. Despite having a dual-purpose main armament she has sacrificed a set of quadruple torpedo-tubes in order to mount a 4inch AA gun.

Quail, a slightly later example of the War Emergency type, in 1942. She has gunnery and air-warning radar and carries her full torpedo-armament.

where of course, and as there was no room within the bridgework the sets were carried in offices stacked on the roof of the galley house, which was carried on the upper deck at the break of the forecastle.

One alteration not yet mentioned was the reduction of the height of the after funnel in ships that carried two funnels. The exact amount cut down varied from ship to ship, but the average amount removed was about four feet; and the drawings of *Ashanti* and *Faulkner* illustrate this feature.

A piece of equipment sometimes carried on the older fleet destroyers from the beginning of 1941 was the HF/DF gear, with the associated aerial carried at the head of a separate pole mast, placed well away from the rest of the rig to avoid interference with its operation; in most cases the HF/DF mast was placed at the forward end of the after deckhouse, as shown in the *Faulkner* and *Icarus*.

18

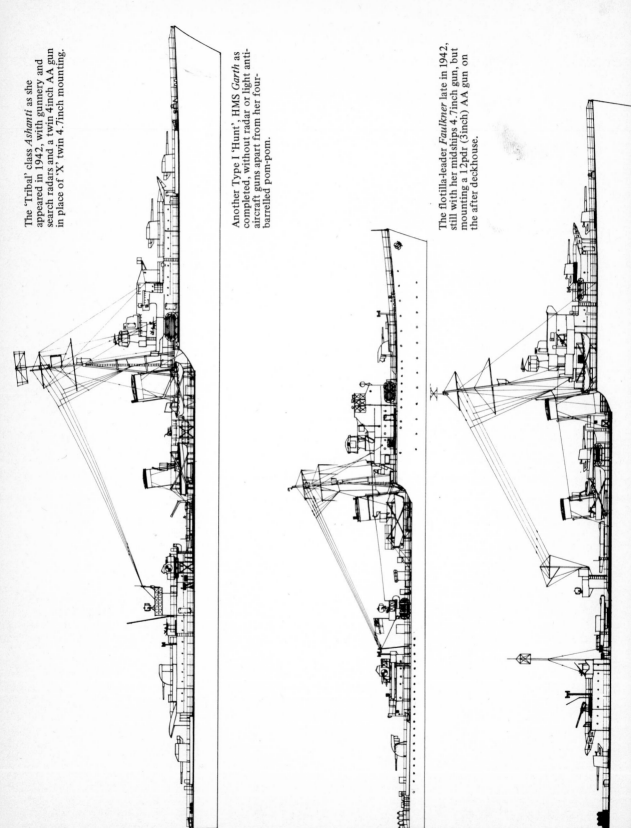

The 'Tribal' class *Ashanti* as she appeared in 1942, with gunnery and search radars and a twin 4inch AA gun in place of 'X' twin 4.7inch mounting.

Another Type I 'Hunt', HMS *Garth* as completed, without radar or light anti-aircraft guns apart from her four-barrelled pom-pom.

The flotilla-leader *Faulkner* late in 1942, still with her midships 4.7inch gun, but mounting a 12pdr (3inch) AA gun on the after deckhouse.

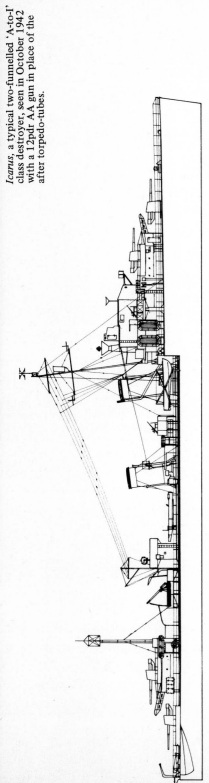

Icarus, a typical two-funnelled 'A-to-I' class destroyer, seen in October 1942 with a 12pdr AA gun in place of the after torpedo-tubes.

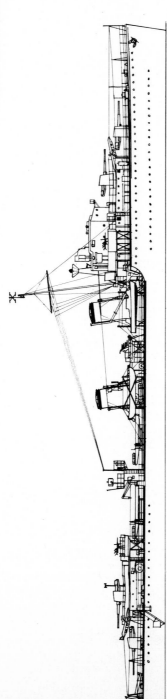

Ithuriel was an ex-Turkish unit similar to the 'H' class. She is seen here late in 1942 with air-warning radar fitted.

All drawings by the Author.

FAR LEFT:
Nubian, one of Thornycroft's 'Tribals' on completion, late in 1938 or early 1939. She also has a tripod mainmast.

Vosper-Thornycroft/NMM

MIDDLE LEFT:
Kipling seen in 1941-42, has only a search radar aerial at the masthead and a 4inch AA gun in place of the after torpedo-tubes.

MoD

LEFT:
The Polish *Piorun,* formerly HMS *Nerissa,* leaving the Clyde at the end of 1940. She has no radar but the after quintuple torpedo-tubes have been replaced by a 4inch AA gun during completion. She still carries TSDS (Two-Speed Destroyer Sweep) aft.

UCS

RIGHT:
Havant, an ex-Brazilian 'H' class boat, seen on 3 May 1940 just before her loss at Dunkirk. She has been completed with that might be termed Stage I modifications: a tripod mainmast to eliminate shrouds, shorter funnels and depth-charges in place of 'Y' 4.7inch gun. She also lacks a director tower on the bridge.

MoD

BELOW:
HMCS *Fraser,* a typical pre-war 'A-to-I' class boat with two tall funnels and a mainmast. It is easy to see how the shrouds would obstruct sky-arcs of anti-aircraft guns. Note also the Two-Speed minesweeping gear on the quarterdeck, another fitting which tended to disappear in wartime.

Author's Collection

Z24 as completed, with a single 15 cm
gun forward and radar aerial on the
bridge. Apart from the heavier look and
bigger funnels the resemblance to
earlier German destroyers was marked.

Druppel

The Narvik Flotilla

GERMAN DESTROYER DESIGN 1936-45

By ANTONY PRESTON

PART 1 Z23-30

The German Navy tried twice in the
space of twenty years to produce a
destroyer with an ultra-heavy armament. In 1916 the four principal
builders, Schichau, Vulcan, Germania
and Blohm & Voss were asked to
tender for 2000-ton destroyers armed
with 15cm (5.9 inch) guns. The series
S113-115, V116-118, G119-121 and
B122-124 was overtaken by events,
and only two were completed by the
time of the Armistice. Despite their
poor performance as seaboats in the
North Sea, due mainly to excessive
topweight *S113* and *V116* were well
regarded by the French and Italian
navies, who took them over as the
Amiral Senes and *Premuda* respectively. This was an indication of the less
demanding conditions in the
Mediterranean, but there was another
practical objection to having such
heavy guns in destroyers. The lively
motion in any sort of seaway made
the handling of any shell weighing
100lbs or more very difficult, and as
fire control in destroyers was rudi-
mentary to say the least, the slow rate
of fire made hitting the target even
harder than with faster-firing guns.

It is therefore all the more puzzl-
ing to see the reappearance of the
15cm gun in German destroyer-
designs produced in 1936. The reason
seems more psychological than mili-
tary, for the development of the first
destroyers for Hitler's rebuilt
Kriegsmarine was more logical. The
1934 Type, numbered *Z1-8* were
armed with the 12.7cm L/50 Model
C34, which compared favourably
with the 4.7inch (12cm) gun in
British and Italian destroyers. On the
other hand the French *contre-
torpilleurs* of the *Fantasque* and

Mogador classes were armed with
13.8cm (5.5inch) guns, and many
German warship designs were originally conceived with a view to operations against France. But above all the
German Navy was worried about the
overwhelming strength of the Royal
Navy, which had 200 destroyers. The
Kriegsmarine was also very weak in
light cruisers for work with the Fleet,
and some senior officers hoped that a
heavily gunned destroyer would
somehow bridge this gap and at the
same time build up the qualitative
strength of the flotillas. This view
does not seem to have been shared by
the majority of destroyer officers,
who favoured more modest designs.

Not that the 1934 Type were
small: *Z1-8* displaced 2170-2232 tons
in standard condition (3100-3156
tons full load), which made them
roughly comparable with their con-
temporaries in the Japanese Navy.
Their likely opponents, the British
'Tribal' class, displaced 1959 tons
standard and 2519 tons full load, and
were about 20ft shorter between per-
pendiculars, and had roughly the
same beam (36.5ft as against 37ft).
But the British designers were much
more cautious in the weight of armament: four twin 4.7inch gun-mount-
ings and only one set of quadruple
torpedo-tubes, whereas the Marineamt
was happy to have five single 12.7cm
guns and two sets of quadruple
torpedo-tubes. In one respect the
German Staff Requirement was more
sound, as the British emphasis on
gunpower in the 'Tribals' ignored the
limited accuracy of destroyer gunfire
as against the well-known efficacy of
torpedo attack. But the weight of
armament in a hull which was little

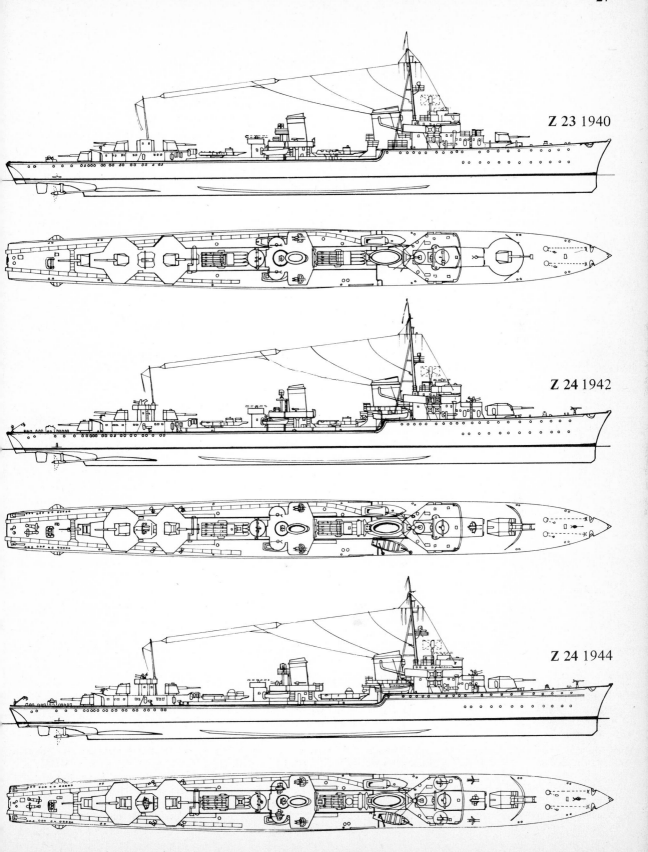

Z 23 1940

Z 24 1942

Z 24 1944

bigger than the 'Tribal' meant a sacrifice of seakeeping qualities. Another factor which is not so obvious is the large discrepancy of about 600 tons in deep load condition between the British and German designs. This accentuated any shortcomings in seaworthiness and affected sea speed and performance.

The Germans exploited to the full recent advances in high-pressure steam, and adopted Wagner boilers operating at a pressure of 70 atmospheres (995lbs psi) 480°C, and Benson boilers operating at 110 atmospheres (1564lbs psi). This was at a time when 500lbs psi, 325°C was considered too adventurous by the Royal Navy, and the Japanese were planning the *Shimakaze's* plant operating at 40 atmospheres (568lbs psi), 400°C. The results looked impressive on paper, for the weight/power ratio went down to 13.8kg/shaft horsepower as against 20kg/shp for a destroyer at the end of the First World War and double that figure only ten years earlier. But in practice a heavy penalty was paid for such a giant stride forward, and the German Navy ruefully joked about their machinery 'developing rickets'. This problem affected major warships as well, but the destroyers were particularly badly hit as their machinery was called upon to make proportionately greater efforts.

The original 1934 Type came into service in 1937-1938 and were immediately followed by the slightly modified 1934A Type, *Z9-16*, which were completed in 1938-39. In the 1936 Type (*Z17-22*) some attempt was made to improve seaworthiness by lengthening the bow. This provided extra buoyancy to offset the overloading of the forward end, which made the bow bury itself in a head sea. It was at this point that the decision was taken to build a new class of super-destroyers, and as their design followed on the heels of *Z17-22* the project was known as the 1936A Type.

The new class followed the general lines of the 1936 Type, a transversely framed hull with the traditional raised forecastle. The boilers were grouped in pairs abreast, in two boiler-rooms leading to a forward uptake and a separate boiler-room serving the after uptake. The torpedo-tubes were disposed between the funnels and between the after funnel and after deckhouse, and the layout of guns was copied from the French *Fantasque* class, but with a twin enclosed turret forward and three single guns aft. The fifth gun on the after superstructure was drier in bad weather than the quarterdeck gun, but its limited arcs made it less valuable and some ships had it removed during the War. In appearance and layout they strongly resembled the earlier destroyer, with big capped funnels and a clipper bow.

The legend displacement was 2570 tons and weights broke down as follows:

	Tons
Hull	889.25
Machinery	799.25
Auxiliary machinery	143.90
Armament	275.00
Fittings	100.25
Feed Water	41.10
Drinking water	64.25
Fuel	257.00
	2570.00

Hull weight was up compared with the previous class, but the weight of machinery was the same, as the installation was identical. Understandably armament weight was up and fuel was increased by nearly 75 tons. Metacentric height remained at 2.89ft.

Although the design was drawn up in the autumn of 1935 and the ships were laid down late in 1938 for completion by the end of 1940 the last ships of the class were held up by wartime shortages.

The extra topweight made them roll heavily, especially after the twin 15cm mounting was installed, but they were good seaboats for their size. The manoeuvrability was only moderately good, but the double rudders gave them a small turning circle. The positioning of the water tanks below the fuel tanks also helped stability, and avoided the need to limit fuel consumption in heavy weather.

MODIFICATIONS

With so few destroyers under construction and a somewhat leisurely pace of building the Germans were more prone to make alterations to their ships. *Z28* was fitted out as a flotilla leader, with 'C' gun replaced by extra accommodation. She was unique in having two single guns forward, and so resembled the older destroyers.

The big twin C38 turret-mounting was delayed in production and so the class was completed with a single C36 shield-mounting on a 'bandstand' in 'A' position. When the turret became available it replaced the single gun, but experience soon showed that too

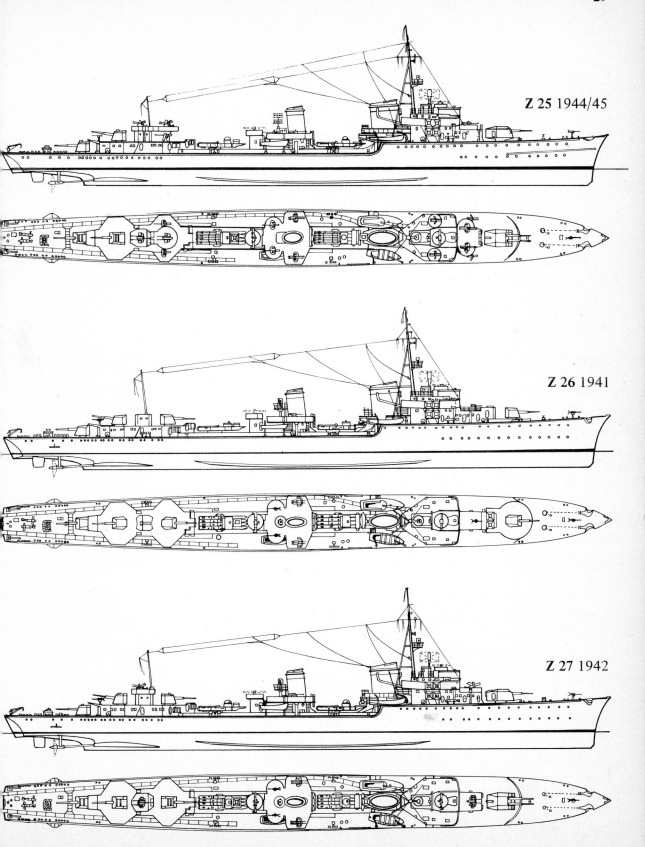

Z 25 1944/45

Z 26 1941

Z 27 1942

much had been attempted. The weight (nearly 100 tons) was too much for the hull and its supporting trunk made for cramped conditions below decks. The dimensions of the 1934 Type, which were barely adequate for a lighter armament, had not been increased nearly enough to allow for the much greater weight of guns. The forward sections were later strengthened, but this did nothing to improve seakeeping.

All except *Z26* (sunk in March 1942) were rearmed with the twin 15cm mounting in 1942-43. Various changes in light armament were made as the war progressed (see illustrations), but typically the ships received twin and single 3.7cm mountings, a quadruple 2cm 'vierling' on the after superstructure, and single 2cm. The 15cm guns carried 120 rounds per gun, whereas the 3.7cm and 2cm guns usually had 2000 rpg.

PARTICULARS

Length:	126.5m (oa), 122.0m (cwl)
	315ft 400ft 3in
Beam:	12m
	39ft 4in
.Draught:	4.6m
	15ft 1in
Machinery:	2-shaft Wagner geared turbines, 70 000 shp
	= 38½ knots; six Wagner boilers
Guns:	Five 15cm/50, three in C36 centre-pivot mountings and two in C38 twin mounting (3x1, 1x2)
	Four 3.7cm Flak-C30
	Four 2cm Fla MG C30 (4x1)
Torpedo Tubes:	Eight 53.cm (2x4), twelve G7a torpedoes carried
Fuel:	750 ts (maximum)
Endurance:	5,000 nautical miles @ 19 knots
Complement:	321

FIRST GROUP	Laid down	Launched	Completed	Builder
Z 23	38	15.12.39	40	Deschimag, Bremen*
Z 24	38	7. 3.40	40	—do—
Z 25	38	16. 3.40	30.11.40	—do—
Z 26	38	2. 4.40	41	—do—
Z 27	38	1. 8.40	41	—do—
Z 28	38	20. 8.40	41	—do—
Z 29	38	15.10.40	25. 6.41	—do—
Z 30	38	8.12.40	15.11.41	—do—

*formerly AG Weser

ABOVE:
Z28, the 'odd man out' of the *Z23*
group. As a flotilla-leader she had a
large deckhouse aft and two single
15cm guns forward

Druppel

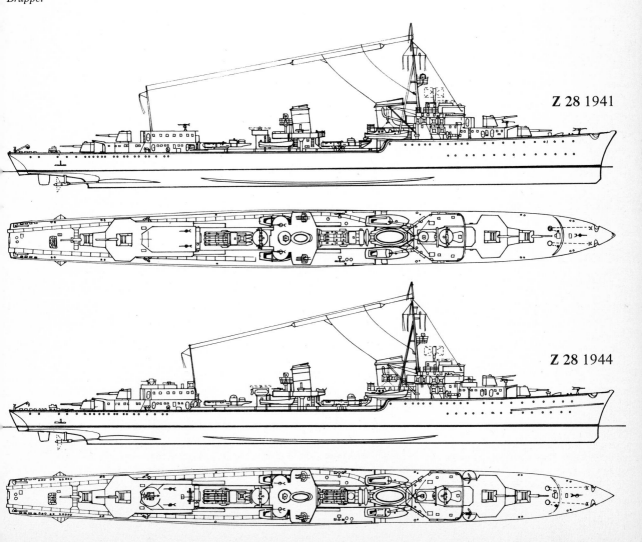

Z 28 1941

Z 28 1944

FATES

Z23: On 1 April 1943 she and *Z24*, *Z32* and *Z37* beat off an attack by Beaufort and Torbeau aircraft 140 miles West of Vigo while escorting the Italian blockade-runner *Pietro Orsoleo* into the Gironde. She was involved in an unsuccessful attempt to cover the breakout of the Italian *Himalaya* on 9-10 April 1943, and in operations in the Bay of Biscay in June and July. Finally damaged by British aircraft off La Pallice and scuttled on 21 August 1944.

Z24: She was transferred with *Admiral Hipper* and *Z26* and *Z30* to Trondheim in March 1942. She took part in an action against the cruiser HMS *Trinidad* on 29 March and against the cruiser *Edinburgh* on 29 April 1942. She rescued *U185* and the survivors of *U564* in the Bay of Biscay on 4 June 1943 and took part in various actions with British air and sea groups in June and July (operations 'Musketry' and 'Seaslug'). She was in action with the cruisers *Glasgow* and *Enterprise* in the Bay of Biscay on 28 December 1943, and again with 'Tribal' class destroyers of the 10th Flotilla on 8-9 June 1944. She was attacked by rocket-firing aircraft off Le Verdon (NW of Ile de Bas) and was driven ashore on 25 August 1944.

Z25: She took part in operations against convoys PQ12 and QP8 in March 1942, and fought in the actions against the cruisers *Edinburgh* and *Trinidad*. She escorted the damaged cruiser *Prinz Eugen* back to Kiel in May 1942. As part of the 6th Destroyer Flotilla, in March 1944 she bombarded Russian positions in the Gulf of Finland and laid mines. She took part in operations in the Gulf of Riga in August and November 1944 and covered the German withdrawal to the West in January-May 1945. She was surrendered to the British in 1945, who handed her over to the French. Renamed *Hoche,* she was broken up in 1956.

Z26: She was transferred to Trondheim with the *Admiral Hipper* in March 1942, and on 29 March she sank SS *Bateau* of PQ13. She was hit by 6inch gunfire from HMS *Trinidad* and sank after 96 survivors had been rescued by *Z24* and *Z25.*

Z27: She took part in Operation 'Rosselsprung' against PQ17 in July 1942, and laid mines off Kanin Nos in October that year. As part of the 8th Flotilla she operated against shipping in the Arctic in October-November 1942 and sank the Russian tanker *Donbass* and subchaser *BO78* on 7 November 1942. She took part in Operation 'Sizilien/Zitronella' with the *Tirpitz* against Spitzbergen in September 1943. Sunk by gunfire from the cruisers *Glasgow* and *Enterprise* in the Bay of Biscay on 28 December 1943.

Z28: She took part in operations against PQ17 in July 1942, and with the *Admiral Hipper* laid mines off Novya Zemlya in September. In March 1944 she bombarded Russian shore positions in the Gulf of Finland and laid mines, and was again in action in the Gulf of Riga in August 1944. She was hit by a Russian bomb off Memel on 23-24 October but was repaired and took part in the withdrawal from the East early in 1945. She was damaged by a mine off Sassnitz and subsequently sunk by British Aircraft (150 casulaties). The wreck was later raised and scrapped.

Z29: She took part in operations against PQ17 in July 1942 and in September laid mines in the Kara Straits and off Novya Zemlya. She took part in Operation 'Regenbogen' against convoy JW51B (the Battle of the Barents Sea) and with the *Friedrich Eckholdt* and *Richard Beitzen* sank the British minesweeper *Bramble*. She was in Operation 'Sizilien/Zitronella' in September 1943 and formed part of the *Scharnhorst's* escort before the Battle of North Cape, 26 December 1943. She fell into American hands in 1945 and was scuttled in the Skagerrak on 16 December 1946.

Z30: She escorted the *Admiral Hipper* to Trondheim in March 1942. She laid mines off the Kara Straits and off Novya Zemlya in September 1942, and again off Kanin Nos in October, and operated against convoys in November. On 31 December 1942 she took part in the disastrous Operation 'Regenbogen' against JW51B. In September 1943 she escorted the *Tirpitz* on Operation 'Sizilien/Zitronella' and was part of the *Scharnhorst's* escort for the last sortie.

RIGHT, ABOVE:
Z25 seen in dock in France, with her forward guns fully elevated.
Navpic

RIGHT, BELOW:
Z26 in Northern waters in early 1942
Druppel

Z 30 1944/45

CLASSIC SHIP MODELS

BELOW
USS *Wilkes-Barre* (CL-103) under construction on my *always very neat* work area, the 'used-to-be' dining room table

BOTTOM
Wilkes-Barre alongside USS *Yorktown* as part of 'The Fighting Lady' diorama, on display at the US Bicentennial Exhibit, at the Philadelphia Naval Base.

Author's photo

The USS WILKES-BARRE

By LAWRENCE SOWINSKI

Larry Sowinski lives in New York and is a member of the New York Model Shipcraft Guild, for whom he edits their journal *The Binnacle.* He has made a large number of diorama models for public exhibition and is the author of a new book on US warship camouflage.

The past several years have seen a major change in the attitude of warship modelling, at least in the United States. Previously, 'anything goes' was commonplace. It used to be rare to see a faithfully reproduced warship model, including even the prize winners at exhibits. Additionally, it was almost dishonorable to be a steam warship modeler. We were the black sheep of most serious modelling clubs (assuming we were allowed to join).

However, we Americans are finally emerging from our cocoons, even though we are decades behind other countries. Britain continues to lead as evidenced by the birth of this magazine.

The increased interest in warship modelling has been generated by the perfecting of plastic molds. One need only to compare the early Airfix kits of HMS *Suffolk* next to their relatively new HMS *Belfast*. A major criticism of plastic warship models continues to be the horribly over-scaled masts, rigging and light guns.

While American plastic companies have released many 'new' warship kits, they are usually just re-issues from the same twenty-five year old molds. The 'new' applies only to the box art and ship's name. These companies bear much of the responsibility for American modellers' liberal use of 'artistic license'. Many novices, myself included, began building a constant scale collection by using plastic kits as three-dimensional blueprints. Details were added by studying pictures from books or magazines, generally only small surface views.

Critical modelling dimensions often had to be taken from guess work data in existing publications. I built thirteen WW2 'Tribals' to a scale length of 355ft instead of 377ft because that was the longest dimension I could find!

Many of these problems are now behind me — primarily because there are so many accurate plans and data readily available. In addition, I now also know how and where to find

whatever else I may need.

One of my latest models, USS *Wilkes-Barre* (CL-103) is a typical example. She was built for display at the US Navy Bicentennial Exhibit at Philadelphia, and *Wilkes-Barre* was chosen because whe was the only *Cleveland* class light cruiser to be named after a Pennsylvania city.

Initially, I began working from a poor set of 'class' plans. While I had an extensive collection of 8in by 10in photos of *Clevelands,* I had next to nothing on CL-103. A fellow 'warship freak', Pat O'Brien, lent me his complete set of plan views of *Wilkes-Barre* undergoing inclining experiments at Camden, NJ. Since these were taken prior to commissioning some equipment was not yet installed, but this official series of 8in by 10in close-ups showed excellent views of the basic superstructure and other topside shapes.

In the meantime, another 'war monger', Bob Morales, lent me a great set of color slides, taken while *Wilkes-Barre* was laid up at the

Philadelphia Naval Base after World War II.

However I still had very little of the ship as 'dazzle' painted, so I purchased several port and starboard views from the National Archives in Washington, DC. At $ 3.25 apiece, I couldn't afford too many of them. Then to my chagrin, I found that Floating Drydock (Philadelphia) carried the *entire* Archives collection of *Wilkes-Barre* for only $ 1.25 a copy: at almost one-third the cost. I now confine my purchases to them. The people at Floating Drydock provided a priceless service; they lent me a set of official plans of *Wilkes-Barre* as in 1946. These plans are being redrawn and will soon be available as part of their extensive warship plans list. This company then proved even more valuable by also supplying me with the official camouflage design sheets for *Wilkes-Barre's* scheme.

I now had more research material with which to build a specific ship, than ever before. Additionally, I had a batch of official photographs of both round- and square-bridged sister ships (from Floating Drydock and the Archives). This included close-ups, aerial and sea level views. These enabled me to pick out small deck fittings and superstructure details not clearly distinguishable in the *Wilkes-Barre* photos.

Because my scale is relatively small (1ft = 516ft) it is simple to reduce large plans to my size without great expense. This also saves the trouble of having to scale everything down. Reductions can be made either photostatically or by negless xerox, but increases in scale cannot be done on negless xerox.

Model building demands constant attention to detail, contours and lines. After I had shaped the hull to *my* satisfaction, Bob Morales 'eyeballed' the stern and flunked it. As usual, he was right. Closer examination of photos showed that I had failed to shape properly the unique reverse contours of the stern.

A quick look at most photos gives the impression that the *Clevelands* had a very simple, high-sided hull. Strong broadside light reflection emphasized this even more, especially in aerial shots. This was caused by the tumblehome, another feature unique to the *Clevelands.* A recent trip to Philadelphia allowed a good photo comparison of the sistership *Springfield's* hull shape with that of the heavy cruiser *Des Moines.* I was able to walk around *Springfield* (inboard ship, next to the pier) as she lay in reserve. Her hull contours were unaffected by the conversion to a guided missile cruiser. By a coincidence, *Springfield* was moored in the same spot in 'Cruiser Row' as *Wilkes-Barre* had been ten years earlier. While CL-103 never saw any post-WW2 service her sistership was extensively modernized and enjoyed a long career. During my latest trip to 'Cruiser Row', I was surprised to discover that *Springfield* had been moved into the inner yard to be stripped for sale. The 'show boat' mooring next to the main gate, previously filled with *Clevelands,* such as *Wilkes-Barre, Topeka* and *Springfield,* is now home for the mighty *Newport News.* This finally brings all three of the world's largest cruisers together, the sisterships *Newport News, Des Moines* and *Salem,* all in reserve.

Norman Friedman tells me that the tumblehome in the *Cleveland* class was intended to raise the metacentric height by lowering the centre of gravity. The increased stability had to be allowed for added topside weight. Initial units carried a fairly small number of light AA, but towards the end of the war, as additional sisters were completed and the early ships were refitted, the *Clevelands* became top heavy. The weighty 40mm twin and quad mounts had replaced most of the light, single 20mms, some of the remaining singles were converted to twin manual mounts.

It must be remembered that the *Clevelands* were designed with an impressive main armament and heavy AA battery at the design stage, all mounted high in the ship. The twin 5in/38 enclosed dual-purpose mounts were placed on the 01 (superstructure) deck for clear fields of AA fire. The *Cleveland* design was the direct result of the previous *Brooklyn* class, but it was wisely decided to abandon the *Brooklyn's* fifth 6in triple turret in favor of two additional 5in/38 twin mounts. This fifth turret had a very limited arc of fire, with no superfiring or AA capability, while the twin 5in mounts (as installed on the *Clevelands*) which replaced this turret, were dual purpose, with wide arcs of AA fire. Thus, while the *Clevelands* carried a lighter main battery of twelve 6in guns as against the *Brooklyns'* fifteen, the number of dual purpose 5in guns was raised from eight to twelve. These DPs saw considerably more action than the main battery.

The official plans I had borrowed

were of *Wilkes-Barre* as rigged in 1946. The appearance differences between August 1944 and this date were minimal and readily discernible in photographs. The most notable modifications included:

a) The forward air defense level was extended to enable a 'walk-around' the forward main battery director.

b) The single 20mm mounts bolted to the wooden 01 deck abaft the bridge were removed and replaced with single 3-pounder saluting guns.

c) The staggered single 20mm mounts on the 01 deck abaft the after control station were replaced by twin 20mm mounts. This was also done to the single 20mm abaft the after funnel (on top of the after control superstructure).

d) The midships twin 40mm mounts and their raised platforms were removed.

e) The single 20mm on the fantail were replaced with twin 40mm in tubs (probably the same 40 mm removed from amidships).

Note: All of these AA modifications were carried out to both the port and starboard positions.

Several square-bridged *Clevelands* (including *Astoria* and *Miami*) were completed with 20mm groups abaft the forward and after superstructure extremities. These where two single 20mm mounts in a raised bandstand on each quarter. Each of these groups were replaced by a twin 40mm mount in an enclosed tub. *Wilkes-Barre* carried these 20mm during her inclining experiments, but they were replaced before commissioning with the standard twin 40mm.

The later units, as well as early ships extensively refitted in late 1944 or 1945, carried the disk-shaped SK2 radar antenna (on the foremast radar platform). However, *Wilkes-Barre* kept her 'as fitted' SK 'bedspring' antenna, until it was removed during de-activation. Only one *Cleveland* carried the SK antenna on the mainmast radar platform, the *Biloxi*.

As noted earlier a number of *Clevelands* saw considerable service after WW2, primarily in the form of guided missile cruisers with flagship duties (*Springfield* served as Comsix with the Mediterranean 6th Fleet).

OPPOSITE, TOP

USS *Wilkes-Barre* out of the Philadelphia Navy Yard, 18 August 1944. She is painted in Measure 32, design 24D. The vertical colors are light grey and dull black. Note the foremast in light grey.

Official USN photo

BELOW

Plan view of USS *Astoria* (CL-90) sistership to CL-103. This is one of a series and was invaluable when building the *Wilkes-Barre*. *Astoria* is wearing the same camouflage design (24D) but to Measure 33 colors, light grey and ocean grey. The mainmast is dull black.

Official USN photo

The *Manchester* was completed post-war with the standard 40mm mounts, but they were soon replaced with twin 3in guns. This distinguished *Manchester* as the only active *Cleveland* class cruiser in the early 1950s. She saw action off Korea in company with the battleship *Missouri*.

Practically every US warship was topheavy by 1945, which explains the removal of as much topside weight as possible. The *Clevelands* were no exception; immediately after the war a number of steps were taken to lighten them. These usually included removal of all the 20mm, several 40mm and either one or both of the heavy catapults, the spotter aircraft and associated equipment.

Nine *Clevelands* were converted to light fleet carriers while still under construction. This became necessary after the heavy carrier losses in the Pacific during 1942. The conversions were intended as stop-gap measures until the *Essex* class large fleet carriers could make their presence felt in impressive numbers. However, these CVLs operated as first line carriers for the entire war, side by side with the big *Essex* class. One of these light carriers, the *Princeton*, was the only war-built fleet carrier to be lost during the entire war. None of the *Clevelands* completed as cruisers were sunk despite heavy engagement, and even the badly damaged *Houston* was brought back.

Some modellers dread working from official plans because they can be difficult to interpret, especially when compared to the redrawn A&A or Floating Drydock plans. However, USN plans offer the advantage of being able to see inside the hull and superstructure decks. Also guesses can be either confirmed or discredited. For example, the prominent stove-pipe winding its way up the forward section of the *Clevelands'* after funnel, ends up to be the smoke vent for burned wastes instead of the galley funnel which we believed it to be. The small deck house on the 01 deck level between the stacks turns out to be the potato storage locker. The round pedestals supporting the quad 40mm mounts each housed a radar equipment room. The captain's cabin is on the starboard side, main deck, immediately forward of the forward starboard side 5in handling rooms. The same cabin on the port side was reserved for guests. Radio central was in the forward superstructure, directly between the forward 5in wing mounts on the 01 deck.

CAMOUFLAGE

Wilkes-Barre was painted up in Measure 32, design 24D. Originally intended for destroyers (D), this pattern was adopted for the *Cleveland* class. As redrawn the master-design carried a light vertical pattern. Designated as Measure 33, it used light gray and ocean gray. This design with light vertical colors was very popular with *Cleveland* class cruisers and was carried by *Astoria, Atlanta, Springfield* and *Topeka*.

This same Measure 33 (light pattern) was changed to a Measure 32 (medium pattern) by substituting dull black in place of ocean gray, while the light color (light gray) was unaffected. Thus the pattern contrast was greatly increased. This was a perfectly acceptable practice and is gone into in greater detail in the official *U.S. Navy Camouflage Instructions*, March 1943 Supplement. The camouflage pattern painted on *Wilkes-Barre* followed the same lines of design 24D as redrawn for the *Cleveland* class. But whoever supervised the application of the dull black patterns was not very precise (nor was he required to be). As a result, some of the curves do not flow smoothly, but instead, in a rather bumpy fashion.

While *Wilkes Barre's* contrast and color range were changed to Measure 32 on the vertical surfaces, the colors on the horizontal and deck surfaces remained the same, a pattern of deck blue and ocean gray. Most deck patterns attempted to fake the ship's actual course, and this was done on *Wilkes-Barre* by painting a pattern on the forecastle to give the impression that the ship was turning to starboard.

It was standard practice not to vary the deck colors, regardless of the vertical color range, be it Measure 33 (light), Measure 32 (medium) or Measure 31 (dark). Even a ship painted in a white and pale blue pattern, (Measure 16) carried the same dark deck blue on its decks as did ships with vertical surfaces painted in navy blue.

Not all *Clevelands* carried patterns. Those units which did were painted up either in Measure 33 (light pattern) or Measure 32 (medium pattern). The only exception that I'm aware of was *Amsterdam*. She commissioned in a Measure 31a pattern carrying a dark range of colors.

Measure 31 and its variant, 31a, were intended as camouflage against aircraft, and applied only to fleet warships. Measure 31, as painted in

Another *Wilkes-Barre* sistership, the *Vicksburg.* The unusual shape of the stern is evident. This is one of the more than fifty *Cleveland* class photos that I was able to refer to for details. Note the cutout for the stern lights. *Vicksburg* is wearing Measure 33, design 6D, and is painted (light to dark) with vertical colors of pale grey, haze grey, navy blue and black boot topping.

Official USN photo

greens on landing ships and land craft, was both an anti-aircraft and anti-surface measure when viewed against a land and foliage background.

Measure 33, with its light colors, was primarily an anti-submarine camouflage. It was considered highly visible to aircraft.

Measure 32 resolved to a medium color and was intended as a general purpose camouflage pattern. It was for this reason that a Measure 33 design was adopted to Measure 32 colors and applied to both *Wilkes-Barre* and her sister *Pasadena.*

For enthusiasts interested in a more complete understanding of USN camouflage, I suggest *United States Navy Camouflage of the WW2 Era.* As co-author I am, no doubt, very biased in making this recommendation. Each chapter is based on official camouflage instructions, in chronological order. Chapter 5 deals with the March 1943 Supplement which was primarily concerned with Measures 33, 32 and 31 (all patterns). No color chips are included, although the full color cover shows the entire range of US Navy wartime paint shades as applied to models, including *Wilkes-Barre.* Despite color corrections and two printers' reruns, the publishers are not able to guarantee the exact color tint throughout the cover's entire press run. This is a problem common to all full color printing. Therefore, it was decided to give comprehensive color descriptions of each paint, as it was introduced by the Navy. Presently, there are *no* commercially available paints that accurately match US Navy tints. Floating Drydock is in the process of preparing a set of paint chips of the most

popular colors.

The model has a number of errors in the camouflage pattern shapes. Despite thorough 'eye-balling', something always manages to slip by unnoticed. When *Wilkes-Barre* comes off exhibition these will be corrected; a sloppy bow numeral has already been repainted.

Floater-net cases and life rafts have been intentionally left off the model and they can be added at a later date. Because of my small scale, I leave off details that may give the model too cluttered a look. As photographed the dull black color appears a little too dark for scale, even though it was actually mixed as a dark blue-gray.

Except for carriers, which used a blue stain on their flight decks, the planked decks of US warships were painted during WW2. There is a slight color or value variation when light reflects on painted wood next to painted steel. Therefore at certain aerial angles, *Wilkes-Barre's* steel forecastle, fantail and turret tops appear to be painted with different deck colors from the planked decks, although the colors are actually the same.

USS *WILKES-BARRE* AT WAR
Unlike some of her sister ships, *Wilkes-Barre* did not see extensive action. The strength of the US Navy was overwhelming by the time she reported to the Pacific, and there weren't many Japanese warships left to shoot at. Those that were still afloat were not so suicidal as to challenge an entire US task force. As a unit of Cruiser Division 17, *Wilkes-Barre* divided her duties between screening the fast carrier forces and shore bombardment. On April 11, 1945, during heavy *kamikaze* attacks she shot down six attacking aircraft. She helped to save the carrier *Bunker Hill* after that ship was terribly damaged by two *kamikazes.*

Like so many of her proud sisters, *Wilkes-Barre* was unceremoniously sold for scrap after years in reserve. She lost the final battle — her enemies were age and obsolescence. But *Wilkes-Barre* finally cheated the razor blade factory; while being towed from Philadelphia to Orange, Texas,

she foundered.

SOURCES FOR US WARSHIP PHOTOS, PLANS, DRAWINGS AND FITTINGS
While American firms may handle a few model builders' steam warship plans, or a couple of kits and a fitting or two, they do not specialize in this era (WW2 to the present day). They are primarily concerned with sail. To almost all US modellers, it's the distinction between sail and steam that actually makes the difference, not the fact that both types may or may not be warships.
Floating Drydock is the only 'one stop' service for enthusiasts of modern American warships. The majority of their items tend to be of the WW2 period, but the range is constantly expanding. They have the largest privately available official plans list. There are two catalogs, both are one dollar each (add 25% for non-US orders). The first includes official plans, redrawn official plans, Chesley drawings, Sumrall drawings (soon to be added), ship model shop plans and kits, camouflage design sheets, photo sets of official models, fittings, nautical publications, prints, tools, etc. The second is exclusively a photo catalog which shows each 8in by 10in photo available in postage stamp size. This enables the buyer to see what he's getting before he places an order. Photos are $1.25 each, about a third of the US National Archives price.

Floating Drydock is also the publisher of *United States Navy Camouflage of the WW2 Era* (based on official instructions). If unavailable locally, it may be purchased directly from Floating Drydock for $6.45 (non-US add 25% for postage and handling).

This company is relatively new, and as such has had some early growing pains which have since been corrected. The quality varies with the original. Several poor photos have been discontinued because of this, which is very unfortunate, for now these same photos are only available from the National Archives for $3.25. This company's biggest assets are quantity, price and delivery time (orders are sent out within 24 hours after request). The Floating Drydock,

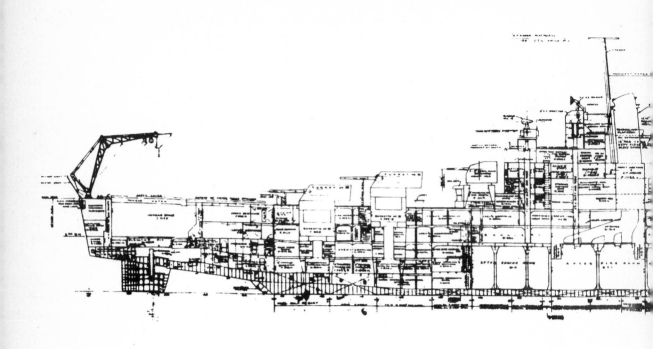

PO Box 16066, Philadelphia, Pennsylvania 19114.

US National Archives, Plans Division offers copies of official plans of all periods up to 1945, but does not include *any* WW2-built ships. There are no lists available. The major portion of this collection deals with early period ships, but there is an interesting number of later ships, especially some of the major ships lost during WW2, expended at Bikini, or scrapped immediately after the war. Quality depends on the original. Written requests must be well detailed and patience is necessary as delivery normally takes two to three months. Cost vary with the size of the plans and the type of reproduction. National Archives, Plans Division (Warships), General Services Administration, Washington, DC 2048.

US National Archieves, Photo Division. Probably the world's largest collection of warship and related photographs. There are no lists available. Written requests must also be well detailed. Your satisfaction depends on the particular staff researcher handling your order. Dedicated individuals are overworked, others are not qualified, while some are not 'motivated'. Generally, both the plans and photo divisions are understaffed. Your initial request will be followed up by a form describing the pictures available. Indicate your choice, enclose remittance (starts at $3.25 for an 8in by 10in) and return. This extensive file of photographs starts at the beginning of photography and stops at the end of 1957. Many are excellent quality, some are not. Some color is available. Normal delivery is usually two months after payment is received. Audio-Visual Branch, General Services Administration, National Archives and Records Services, Washington, DC 20408.

Naval Photographic Center, (photos only) covers the period from the beginning of 1958 up until the present. No lists are available, written requests must also be well detailed. Efficient, but terribly understaffed. Reasonable prices start at $1.25 for an 8in by 10in, but there may be an additional charge for research. Color transparencies are available. Commanding Officer, Naval Photographic Center, Department of the Navy, Anacostia, District of Columbia.

US Navy Printing and Publications — official plans. This is where all the other plans are, *if* they're still in existence. They're very understaffed (one person) and searches take a considerable amount of time. Six months plus, is not uncommon. Of course, many modern plans are classified and as such, are unavailable. Prices tend to be very high, some are off of rather poor microfilm originals. Write brief, but detailed requests. Official Plans, US Navy Printing & Publications, Washington Navy Yard, Washington, DC 20390.

Naval History Division has some very capable people who can be of great help to individuals trying to find material on US Navy ships. However, they suffer from the common problem of too large a workload for too

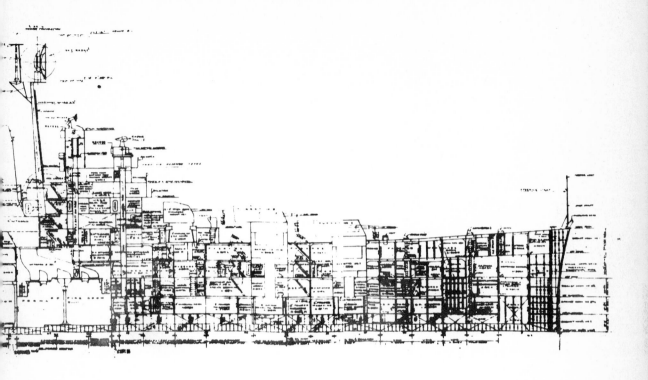

small a staff. Make inquiries brief and to the point. Avoid 'laundry lists'. At the very least they'll be able to tell you where else to write, although it'll probably be a re-hash of the sources I've already mentioned. Naval History Division, Navy Historical Center, Washington Navy yard, Washington, DC 20390.

Except for the *Missouri,* very few US Navy warships have been the subject of model builders. Declassification of confidential materials and companies like Leeward Publications (*Ship's Data* series) and Floating Drydock are doing much to change this. Many fine examples can now be seen at local and national exhibits.

The official plans of the *Atlanta* (CL-104), sister of the *Wilkes-Barre.* Plans like these from official sources often reproduce badly either because the originals are in poor condition or — as here — because they are copied on to very small negatives.

US Archives, by courtesy of Alan Raven

Each issue of *Warship* will devote 4–6 pages exclusively to warship photographs. These will be drawn — initially at least — from the enormous holdings of the Popperfoto/Conway Picture Libraries, which probably form Europe's largest commercial photographic archives. This group is made up of a large number of private collections and smaller picture libraries which have been purchased over the years, and the warship material is vast in both numbers and variety. To give some indication of the range of subjects, the collections can be divided into the following categories:

Ship portraits: Chronologically, these go back almost to the beginnings of photography (there are certainly many from the 1870s) and cover even the smallest navies, and because Popperfoto is still expanding, photographs of the latest ships are constantly added to the collection.

On-board shots and details: Possibly these will be of greatest interest to modelmakers since in many cases whole series exist for one ship. These were mainly taken by newspaper or magazine cameramen who for safety's sake took far more photographs than

were necessary for the particular article they were illustrating. In some cases none were ever published, but even where one or two reached the public eye the rest of the series was simply stored. Again the range is enormous – guns, bridge equipment, radar gear (where it escaped wartime censorship), naval aircraft, and so on. **Action shots:** Some of the Popperfoto collections were originally from news agencies and so there is much to illustrate the war at sea, particularly in the Second World War. Many famous pictures, such as the Planet News set on the sinking of the *Ark*

Royal, are now within the Popperfoto domain, and the news-orientated nature of the collections record many unusual and forgotten incidents of recent naval history.
Related subjects: These include shipbuilding (one set is as early as 1870) and fitting out, naval ports, fleet reviews, and naval personalities.

Warship Pictorial

A rare sight, a French battle squadron in Grand Harbour, Malta, with only three British warships in sight. The ship on the right is the *Justice* with the *Democratie* or the *Verite* on the left. The two battleships in the background appear to be the *Patrie* and *Republique;* on the far right can be seen the battle-cruiser *Indefatigable,* the armoured cruiser *Euryalus* and the light cruiser *Gloucester.* The wearing of funnel bands by the British ships dates the photograph between 1909 and 1913. Any further information about the occasion of this French visit to Malta is welcome.
CPL. W/1/003

44

LEFT, ABOVE:
The launch of the Victorian turret-ship HMS *Sans Pareil* in May 1887. She was the sister of the ill-fated *Victoria*.
CPL. W/1/004

LEFT, BELOW
The German central battery ship *Hansa* completing in 1870. Rated as an iron-clad corvette, she was armed with eight 21cm/19 cal breechloaders and had a speed of 12 knots.
CPL. W/1/005

THIS PAGE, ABOVE:
Between December 1907 and February 1909 the US Navy's 'Great White Fleet' circumnavigated the world to show the flag. The pre-dreadnought *Alabama* is seen here in January 1908, coaling at Castries, St Lucia in the West Indies. Her design was based on that of the British *Majestic* class, a fact reflected in her appearance.
CPL. W/1/006

THIS PAGE, BELOW:
On 22 May 1919 the ex-Austro-Hungarian battleships *Erzherzog Franz Ferdinand* (left) and *Tegetthoff* (right) were handed over to the Italians at Venice for scrapping, to comply with the peace treaty.
CPL. W/1/007

THIS PAGE, ABOVE
An eight-barrelled 2pdr (40mm) pom-pom aboard the aircraft carrier HMS *Illustrious* in the summer of 1940.

CPL. W/1/008

THIS PAGE, MIDDLE:
Loading shells for one of the *Illustrious'* 4.5inch AA mountings.

CPL. W/1/009

THIS PAGE, BELOW
A rare action shot of the French battle-cruiser *Strasbourg* getting under way to escape during the British attack on Mers-el-Kebir on 3 July 1940. Note her main armament of eight 13inch (330mm) guns trained on the beam ready to open fire.

CPL. W/1/010

RIGHT:
The Royal Navy's 'County' class DLG *Glamorgan* in April 1976. Her 'B' 4.5inch twin gunhouse has been replaced by four Aerospatiale Exocet MM38 surface-to-surface missiles.

C & S Taylor

FAR RIGHT:
A destroyer of the Russian 'Krivak' class, the *Storozhevoy,* seen passing through the English Channel in April 1976. She carries four SSN-10 surface-to-surface missiles forward, two twin SAN-4 launchers for surface-to-air missiles, two 12-barrelled A/S rocket-launchers forward and four 76mm guns aft. In addition she carries quadruple torpedo-tubes amidships. The radar sets visible are Head Net 'C', Pop Group, Owl Screech and Don.
     The 'Krivak' class number at least nine units and they are propelled by gas turbines.

CPL. W/1/011

THE FIRST
TOWN CLASS
1908-31

HMS *Birmingham* in 1922 with all her
wartime modifications, tripod mast,
range clock, searchlight platforms, etc.

*National Maritime Museum (NMM)/
Richard Perkins Collection.*

PART 1

David Lyon is a research assistant in the Department of Ships at the National Maritime Museum, Greenwich. He has spent many years working on ships' technical records and has compiled a comprehensive guide to the Museum's Denny Collection of plans and records. He is the author of a Warship Profile on HMS *Cossack* and co-author of another (with David Brown) on HMS *Illustrious*. He is also co-author (with his brother Hugh) of a forthcoming book on warships of World War II.

By David Lyon

No other warship type has a more
complicated history than the cruiser,
and none is so difficult to define.
There have been cruisers which came
near to battleships in size and armament, while others have been no
more than extra-large destroyers.
These two opposite trends, represented at their extremes by the battlecruisers and the 'scouts' of the early
years of this century, have rarely
produced totally satisfactory ships.
Unless battlecruisers were given
adequate armour and weapons they
could not stand up against battleships,
but once they had been given such
protection and armament they
became battleships themselves. The
'scouts' on the other hand proved too
large and expensive to be successfully
employed with destroyers, and too
small and fragile to perform the
normal duties of a cruiser.

The traditional cruiser-duties were
those of a maid-of-all-work, the true
general purpose ship.[1] A cruiser
should be able to go anywhere and do
anything, particularly trade-protection
and scouting for the battlefleet. The
cruiser was the smallest ocean-going
warship and the largest ship which
could be built in large numbers. Such
ships needed a balanced combination
of weapons, speed and protection to
complement good endurance and
sea-keeping capabilities. Although
cruisers should make good commerce
raiders, and therefore would be useful
to the weaker naval power, they were
above all the chief enforcers of sea
supremacy, the most active element
of the forces of the predominant
naval power. It is not surprising,
therefore, that the Royal Navy has
produced so many excellent cruiser

designs, and few of those have been
better or more successful than the
group of ships known as the 'Towns'
which rendered such sterling service
during the First World War.

The 'Towns' served in every major
theatre of the naval war and took
part in every kind of action. They
were not a class, but a group of
classes, representing a steady improvement in seagoing and fighting ability
which ended with arguably the best
cruiser design of the First World War
the *Chester*. I intend in this series to
describe the evolution of this design
and to pay particular attention to the
later members of the group, those in
which armament and protection were
altered to produce a more effective
fighting ship.

PREHISTORY OF THE 'TOWNS'

In the opening years of the
twentieth century British cruiser
design tended towards the extremes
already mentioned. At one end of
the scale a series of armoured cruisers
steadily increased in size and strength
in a progression which culminated in
the building of the first battlecruisers.
At the other extreme a series of light
cruisers (officially called 3rd Class
cruisers) ended with the 'Gem' class,
though one of these, the *Amethyst*,
showed the way to future improvements by successfully trying out the

1. Originally, of course, a 'cruiser' was
simply a ship detached for independent
work, usually commerce-protection or
harassment of enemy commerce. The
ship-types which normally carried out
such duties were the frigate and the sloop,
but in the late nineteenth century the
word was applied to their steam-powered
successors. The last frigate on the Navy
List was HMS *Raleigh*, but she was re-
classified as a cruiser in 1889.

THIS PAGE, ABOVE:
HMS *Falmouth* on trials in 1911. The
6inch guns are more prominent than
the 4inch in the preceding class.

NMM/Richard Perkins Collection

THIS PAGE, BELOW:
This 1927 view of *Yarmouth* illustrates
the changes made in wartime. Bridgework was enlarged, a tripod foremast
was added and a tall searchlight tower
aft. After the Armistice the after 6inch
gun was removed and deckhouses were
added on the quarterdeck.

NMM/Richard Perkins Collection

RIGHT:
Three *Birmingham* class cruisers on a
sweep in the North Sea in 1917. The
two nearest ships have 'baffles' fitted
on the foretopmast in an attempt to
fool enemy rangefinding.

P A Vicary

steam turbine. (For the details of the 'Gems' and following classes see Table 1). Medium cruisers (2nd Class) were represented by the *Challenger*, the last of her size to be built for some time.

For a time the Royal Navy dabbled in ultra-light cruisers, the 'Scouts'. These were really too light to be considered as cruisers at all 'having rather more of the large destroyer ... about them'.[2] They were followed by the *Boadicea* class, a larger development, reverting to the size and type of gun of the 'Gems' but retaining the higher speed of the 'Scouts'. Subsequent ships of the type had a better armament, but were still too small to be entirely satisfactory as cruisers. To be fair, their main purpose was to act as flotilla leaders for destroyers rather than act as ocean cruisers.

THE FIRST 'TOWNS'

The necessary increase in size came with the *Bristol* class, the first of four classes of cruisers named after British town and cities. The design was drawn up in 1908, when the *Boadicea* was still building. With nearly 1000 extra tons of displacement the designers had the choice of adding to speed, armament or protection. In the event the 25 knots of the previous light cruisers was retained, but an armoured deck and conning tower were added, while two 6inch guns supplemented the ten 4inch which armed the later ships in the *Boadicea* group.

Though on the whole satisfactory the class had a poor armament for its size (a complaint voiced in the 1911 *Brassey's Naval Annual*). This was remedied in the succeeding class, the

Weymouths , which had an homogeneous armament of 6inch guns and also a longer forecastle which improved their seagoing qualities.

With the next class, the *Chathams,* this improvement in armament was complemented by a great step forward in protection, the addition of a side belt. Experience with the 'Scouts' had demonstrated that the clipper/ram bow was superior at sea to the straight ram of the first two 'Town' classes. The graceful curve of the clipper/ram became the most prominent recognition feature distinguishing the later 'Towns' from the predecessors.

Besides the three *Chathams* built for the Royal Navy another two similar vessels, *Sydney* and *Melbourne,* were ordered from British yards for the Australian Government. They were to form part of the 'Australian Squadron' intended for the defence of Australia, but were also part of a comprehensive scheme of Imperial Defence decided on at the 1909 Imperial Conference. A third member of the class, HMAS *Brisbane,* was to be built in an Australian yard with British assistance. The turbines for this ship were ordered from Vickers in April 1914 but she was not completed till November 1916.

The *Birminghams,* the class which followed the *Chathams,* were nearly identical to their predecessors, except that their armament was augmented by an extra 6inch gun. The fourth ship ordered for the Australians, the *Adelaide,* was completed in an Australian yard after the end of the war. Though she was originally intended to be similar to the *Birmingham* the design was changed, and the

ship that finally appeared was different in many details, and will not be considered here.

There was, however, another later addition to the 'Town' group which was in time for the war. Two cruisers building for Greece were taken over in early 1915. They differed very little from the 'Towns' except in their armament of 5.5inch guns, and in the fact that one of the two, the *Chester,* was completely oil-fired. As this made the *Chester* perhaps the finest representative of the whole group of 'Towns' it is worth investigating the origin of these Greek ships in more detail before passing to to a more detailed consideration of the design and construction of the whole group.

2. *Light Cruisers (1912-1920)*, page 2. This useful booklet was published internally by the Admiralty as part of a history of wartime construction, and only came into the public domain in 1964.

BALKAN QUARRELS AND BRITISH SHIPYARDS

The decade before the First World War was dominated by the greatest naval arms race of all time. It was this mainly Anglo-German competition which had produced the successive annual programmes of which the *Bristols, Weymouths, Chathams* and *Birminghams* were part. However this was not the only warship-building struggle of that troubled decade. South American republics squandered huge sums on dreadnoughts, and more serious rivalries in the Balkans produced lucrative contracts for the world's shipyards. As Great Britain was the world's leading shipbuilder the lion's share of these orders went to her yards.

In 1914 a number of ships were building in Britain for the two participants in the fiercest and most important of the lesser naval rivalries. Since the time, 90 years earlier, when Daniel Brent had built armed paddle steamers at Rotherhithe for the Greeks who were fighting to free their country from Ottoman rule, there had been tension between Greece and Turkey. In 1911 matters began to come to a head. Italy despoiled Turkey of Libya and the Dodecanese, while Greece (the only one of the allies to possess a navy) combined with the other Balkan nations to drive Turkey out of Europe. When war broke out in 1912 the few skirmishes at sea had little effect on Turkey's defeat, nor on her subsequent partial recovery when the other Balkan states combined against Bulgaria. However, a powerful navy seemed as essential for Turkey's sur-

vival as it would be for revenge. The new revolutionary government of the Young Turks ordered two powerful battleships from British yards.[1]

Greece had a large merchant marine, a long exposed coastline, and a capital vulnerable to bombardment from the sea, and so she had no choice but to respond by naval expansion. The only question was whether to answer battleships by battleships or to build a greater number of small ships. The Greek Navy's Chief of Staff was a British officer, Rear Admiral Sir Mark Kerr (the Turks were also being advised by a British Admiral!). He put forward an original and futuristic scheme for a fleet of torpedo craft; destroyers and submarines to sink the enemy capital ships, backed by seaplanes for reconnaissance, and by cruisers to deal with hostile light forces.

Admiral Kerr's ideas were rejected, and a battlecruiser was ordered from Germany.[2] He must, however, have inspired the order for two light cruisers and four destroyers placed in Britain in 1914. The order went to the Coventry Syndicate, a relatively new armament organisation which linked shipbuilders and steel manufacturers (John Brown & Co, the Fairfield Shipbuilding and Engineering Co, and Cammell Laird & Co) with an armament firm (the Coventry Ordnance Works). This organisation had been created to rival the great Vickers and Armstrong groupings.

The six vessels were still building when Britain declared war on Germany in August 1914, and all were eventually taken over for the Royal Navy. The destroyers, similar to the Admiralty 'M' type, became the *Medea,*

Melampus, Medusa and *Melpomene.* Both cruisers had been ordered from Cammell Laird's, and had been given their yard numbers *809* and *811. 809* was launched with the name *Antinavarhos Kountoriotis* (sometimes transliterated as *Antinaurkos Condouriotis*) the name of a nautical hero of the Greek War of Independence. It is believed that the second ship was to be named *Lambros Katsonis,* but she was taken over before launching and no confirmation has been found for this name in Admiralty records.

During the early months of the war the Greek government continued to pay the instalments on these ships, but by early 1915 fighting in France had bogged down in the unprofitable stalemate of trench warfare, and a new Trafalgar had failed to materialise in the North Sea. The war was obviously lasting longer than expected, and productive capacity could no longer be wasted in building up other countries' navies. As part of a general change in armaments policy the Admiralty Director of Contracts wrote to the Coventry Syndicate announcing that HM Government had decided to take over the two cruisers, together with a supply of thirty-eight 5.5inch guns and their

---

1. See Richard Hough's *The Big Battleship* for a lively account of some aspects of the Turco-Greek conflict, and the subsequent history of the battleships.

2. The *Salamis;* she was never completed because of the outbreak of European war in 1914, but her guns (ordered from America) equipped a class of British monitors.

ABOVE:
The *Chester* in 1918, refitted with a
tripod and the other standard wartime
additions. She and *Birkenhead* could
be distinguished by having an extra gun
on either side abaft the funnels and the
shape of the 5.5inch gun's shield
differed from the 6inch in earlier ships.

Imperial War Museum (IWM)

BELOW:
The *Chester* lying alongside the battle-
cruiser *Inflexible* at Sheerness in 1919.

IWM

HMAS *Brisbane* in 1919. Her anti-aircraft gun can be seen between the funnels and mainmast.

P A Vicary

ammunition. At the same time action was taken to obtain building specifications and drawings of both cruisers, which were to be renamed *Birkenhead* and *Chester.* These names were singularly appropriate, as both were built at Birkenhead, and Chester is only a few miles away from there.

A note on nomenclature: To avoid confusion I have referred to the 'Towns' as 'cruisers' or 'light cruisers'. In fact all four classes were officially termed '2nd Class' cruisers when ordered; sometimes the word 'protected' was used to indicate the fact that they all had armoured decks, and the later classes had side armour. Despite this protection they were not 'armoured cruisers', a term reserved for heavier ships. In 1912 the whole system of cruiser nomenclature was changed, and all the smaller cruisers were re-classified as 'light cruisers'.

In the Admiralty records which were the main sources for this study there is little uniformity in the naming of the different 'Town' classes; in a few instances the group is referred to as the 'Cities' instead. The first class, although usually referred to as the *Bristols,* is occasionally called the *Glasgow* class. The second class is referred to without discrimination (on at least one occasion in the same document) as the *Falmouths* and the *Weymouths,* though the latter name seems to have won more general acceptance since. The third class is the most confusing of all, initially described as the 'New *Bristols'* or 'Colonial Cruisers' (a reference to the Australian members of the class). The name on the 'Cover' for the class[1] is

Melbourne, used as the designation for the whole class, British and Australian. When the British ships are referred to they are sometimes described as the *Chathams,* sometimes the *Dublins* and sometimes the *Southamptons. Brisbane,* being built later and not in Britain is usually not held to be a full member of the class. Fortunately the fourth class present few problems as they seem to have been the *Birmingham* from the start. *(To be continued)*

---

1. The 'Cover' is the bound file of correspondence, memoranda and other documents concerned with design, building and subsequent alterations to a ship or a class kept by the department of the DNC (Director of Naval Construction). The 'Covers' for all the 'Towns' group are now held by the National Maritime Museum.

TABLE I BRITISH AND GERMAN LIGHT CRUISER DEVELOPMENT 1900–1914

Year Completed	Class & No. of Ships	Length(pp) x beam	Armament	Armour	Displace-ment	Design HP	Speed (Knots)
1900–4	*Gazelle* (10)	344½ft x 39–40ft	10 – 4.1in, 2 – 18in TT	2in deck	2645–2715	8500	20
1902	CHALLENGER (1)	355ft x 56ft	11 – 6in, 8–12pdr, 6 – 3pdr, 2 – 18in TT	3in deck	5915	10000	20
1903	'GEM' CLASS (4)	360ft x 40ft	12 – 4in, 8 – 3pdr, 2 – 18in TT	2in deck	3000	9800	21¾
1904	FORWARD (2)	360ft x 39ft	9 – 4in, 2 – 14in TT	2in amidships belt 1½–5/8in deck	2850	16500	25
	SENTINEL (2)	360ft x 40ft	9 – 4in, 2 – 14in TT	1½–5/8in deck	2895	17500	25
	PATHFINDER (2)	370ft x 38¾ft	9 – 4in, 2 – 14in TT	1½–5/8in deck	2940	16500	25
	ADVENTURE (2)	374ft x 38¼ft	9 – 4in, 2 – 14in TT	2in deck	2670	16000	25
1904-7	*Bremen* (7)	364½ft x 34½ft	10 – 4.1in, 2 – 18in TT	2in deck	3250	abt. 11500	23
1907	*Konigsberg* (1)	378ft x 44ft	10 – 4.1in, 2 – 18in TT	2in deck	3400	13200	24
1906	*Nurnberg* (2)	385ft x 44ft	10 – 4.1in, 2 – 18in TT	2in deck	3550	12000–14000	23/24
1907	*Stettin* (1)	385ft x 44ft	10 – 4.1in, 2 – 18in TT	2in deck	3550	21000	25
1908–9	BOADICEA (2)	385ft x 41ft	6 – 4in, 4 – 3pdr, 2 – 18in TT	NIL	3300	18000	25
1908	*Dresden* (2)	388ft x 43ft	10 – 4.1in, 2 – 18in TT	2in deck, 2 1/3–3in amidships belt	3650	13500–15000	24/25
1909–10	BLANCHE (2)	385ft x 41½ft	10 – 4in, 4 – 3pdr, 2 – 21in TT	NIL	3300	18000	25
	Kolberg (4)	428ft x 46ft	12 – 4.1in, 2 – 18in TT	2in deck, 2 1/3 – 3in belt	4350	20000–31000	25/27
	BRISTOL (5)	430ft x 47ft	2 – 6in, 10 – 4in, 4 – 3pdr, 2 – 18in TT	2in deck	4800	22000	25
1900–11	WEYMOUTH (4)	430ft x 48½ft	8 – 6in, 4 – 3pdr, 2 – 21in TT	2in deck	5250	22000	25
1911–12	ACTIVE (3)	385ft x 41½ft	10 – 4in, 4 – 3pdr, 2 – 21in TT	NIL	3440	18000	25
	CHATHAM (5)	430ft x 48¾ft	8 – 6in, 4 – 3pdr, 2 – 21in TT	3in belt	5400	22000	25
	Breslau (4)	455ft x 43½ft	12 – 4.1in, 2 – 20in TT	2¾in belt	4550	25000	27/28
1913	BIRMINGHAM (3)	430ft x 49¾ft	9 – 6in, 4 – 3pdr, 2 – 21in TT	3in belt	5400	22000	24¾
1914	ARETHUSA (8)	450ft x 39ft	2 – 6in, 6 – 4in, 4 – 21in TT	2½in belt	3530	30000	30
	Karlsruhe (1)	468ft x 45ft	12 – 4.1in, 2 – 20in TT	2½in belt	4900	26000	28/29

British ships are in CAPITALS, Germans in *italics*

HMAS *Sydney* alongside in 1914, flying the Australian Jack. The pole foremast with its small control position was typical of the *Southampton* class before the war.

P A Vicary

THE INTRODUCTION OF THE SCREW PROPELLER INTO THE ROYAL NAVY

by DAVID BROWN

Reprinted from the *Transactions of the Institute of Naval Architects* by permission of the I.N.A.

David Brown is a member of the Royal Corps of Naval Constructors, and is working on a history of the 19th century Royal Navy.

During the early 1840s two great technical changes occurred in the Royal Navy: the introduction of the screw propeller and the arrival of the first iron ships. These changes were due to the enthusiasm of the Board of Admiralty led by Thomas, Earl of Haddington with the Rt Hon H T L Corry, MP as First Secretary and Sir George Cockburn as the senior naval member. This article tells of the screw propeller and one of its inventors, Petit Smith aided by the Inspector of Machinery at the Admiralty, Thomas Lloyd, later a Vice-President of the INA.

From the end of the eighteenth century there had been many proposals to use a screw to drive a ship. Of these, the most successful was that of Mr Shorter, whose propeller, turned by eight men at the capstan, drove the transport *Doncaster* for two miles across Gibraltar Bay at 1½ knots. Despite an enthusiastic report by Admiral Bickerton this device was not further developed.

During the first decades of the nineteenth century the Admiralty, conscious of the overwhelming superiority of the Royal Navy in conventional sailing warships, was anxious to avoid encouraging innovation which might lessen the value of this asset. During the 1830s the position changed with the increasing strength of the French and Russian navies and the growing value of the paddle steamer. But the practical deficiencies of the paddler, particularly as a warship, encouraged the search for alternatives.

In 1836 two great men, Ericsson and Smith, both took out patents for screw propulsion. As well as inventive genius, these men had the practical skill and the determination required to bring their invention into service. The Swedish-born engineer, Ericsson, then living in London was the first to offer a demonstration to the Admiralty. He had completed a 45ft launch, the *Frances B Ogden,* in April 1837 and after successful trials in which she reached a speed of 10 knots and towed a 140-ton schooner at 7 knots, Ericsson arranged to tow the Admiralty barge from Whitehall to Woolwich. The distinguished guests, including the reactionary Surveyor, Sir William Symonds, were surprisingly unimpressed.

Ericsson was told that the results were disappointing but no explanation was offered. Later, it appeared that Symonds believed that a propulsor at the stern was certain to lead to directional instability. Some paddlers with the wheels well aft of amidships had been hard to steer and the *Frances B Ogden,* with propellers abaft the rudder could have had problems. It may have been that Ericsson was suspected of concealing such problems by using the Admiralty barge as a drogue. In disgust Ericsson left the country for a successful career in the United States.

The other inventor, Francis Petit Smith, was born in Hythe on February 9, 1808 and though he earned his living as a sheep farmer he was always interested in problems of ship propulsion. He took out his first patent on 31 May 1836 and was able to demonstrate a working model to Sir John Barrow, the very powerful Secretary of the Admiralty.

In February 1837, Smith completed a 6-ton launch, 34ft long which he called the *Francis Smith,* which was fitted with a wooden propeller in the form of two complete turns of a single helix. During her trials on the Paddington canal half the propeller was broken off and the boat went faster. Smith then designed a new screw with one turn. Since opponents allged that the screw was suitable only for river use, Smith took his little launch to Hythe and back. The return trip, in heavy seas, much impressed eye witnesses and official reports from Coastguards to the Admiralty led to an official trial in March 1838. As a result, the introduction of the screw into the RN was deemed a 'not improbable contingency'. Smith was asked for a demonstration on a larger scale and, as a result he borrowed the money to build the *Archimedes* of 237 tons. She was completed in 1839 and after trials and a few teething troubles ended up with a two-start screw of half a turn in length.

The *Archimedes* arrived at Dover in April 1840 for a series of races against the cross channel packets, then operated by the Royal Navy. These races culminated in trials against the *Widgeon,* the fastest paddler in the service. The *Archimedes* was narrowly beaten but since she was the bigger ship and had less power the result was rightly regarded as a triumph for the screw. The Admiralty trials officer, Captain Chappel and Thomas Lloyd, in their detailed and encouraging report, reported that the screw was a success but that the step-up spur gearing was too noisy for a passenger ship. They saw the main use of the screw as being in warships where it interfered less

PARTICULARS OF THE SHIPS

	Propulsor	Length	Beam	Tonnage (bm)	Dispt (tons)	Area of Mid Sec	Draught f.a.	mean
		ft. ins.	ft. ins.				ft ins	ft ins
RATTLER	Screw	176 6	32 8	867	1112	281.8	11 9	12 11
ALECTO	Paddle	164 0	32 8	800	?	281.8	12 0	12 7

with sailing, improved the power of the broadside guns and made boarding easier. By May 1840 the Board had decided to build a screw steamer for the Royal Navy.

After some discussion of alternatives, the prototype steam warship, later named *Rattler,* was ordered on December 14 1840. During that year, Isambard Brunel had carried out an elaborate series of trials with the *Archimedes*, as a result of which he persuaded his directors to change the design of the *Great Britain* to screw propulsion. In consequence, this great engineer was engaged in July 1841 by Sir Edward Parry as a consultant on the development of the machinery and propeller of the *Rattler*. Unfortunately, his terms of reference were far from clear and overlapped those already given to Petit Smith. The Admiralty files for the next two years are full of letters from these gentlemen complaining about each other and about Admiralty delays. Not to be outdone, Sheerness Dockyard, the builders of *Rattler,* responded with complaints about Brunel's delay in supplying drawings.

Hurt feelings apart, one is impressed in reading these files by the sense of urgency and enthusiasm for the project. The picture of a reactionary and incompetent Admiralty given by biographers of Brunel is very one-sided. Only the Surveyor was hostile and even he did little to oppose. There were real technical problems in this new propulsion system which took time and discussion to resolve. The main arguments centred around the stern lines of the *Rattler* and luckily it was decided to lengthen the run by 12ft which improved the flow into the propeller.

HMS *Rattler* carried out her first proving run on 30 October 1843 and a week or so later reached 8¾ knots in the presence of both Brunel and Smith. She ran her first race against the paddler *Polyphemus,* a half-sister, and won. She then went back to Sheerness for various alterations, including coppering the bottom at Brunel's suggestion.

Early in February 1844, serious trials began and *Rattler* soon reached 9¼ knots with a two-bladed Smith screw. Some 3-bladed screws and 2-bladed screws of different diameters were tried with less success. In March a 4-blader by Bennet Woodcroft, who claimed prior patent rights, was tried, followed by runs with various Smith designs until July. There was then a break until October during which the belt drive may have been replaced by gears.

From October onwards, an assortment of screws by Sunderland, Steinman and Hodgson followed. By January 1845, 32 different propellers had been tried; the Smith two-bladed design of 1ft 1inch diameter, 11ft pitch and a length of 1ft 3in proved the most successful. This lengthy series of trials was an essential part of the development of screw propulsion and not, as so often represented by non-technical writers, a deliberate delay by the Admiralty. There were many claims which could only be tested on the ship.

Thomas Lloyd also tried the effect of moving the shortest propeller from one end of the aperture to the other both with and without blanking off the remainder. No conclusive results were obtained from these trials.

RATTLER v ALECTO

The famous competition against the *Alecto,* a paddle half-sister, began on March 30, 1845. The trials were valuable both technically and to convince the remaining doubters, but their Lordships were already convinced. They had already ordered seven screw frigates and some smaller vessels between February 1844 and March 1845, and were about to start the first screw battleships.

Nominal horse power was a geometrical fiction akin to the old RAC rating and, as will be seen, *Rattler* had much greater actual power. Indicated power was measured on both ships and, thanks to Lloyd, £100 was well spent on a mechanical thrust meter for *Rattler*.

At 0554 on a still, calm morning these historic trials began with a race under steam alone from the Nore to Yarmouth. Nearly nine hours later, *Rattler* reached the finish, followed 20 minutes later by *Alecto.* The screw ship had averaged 9.2 knots and the paddler 8.8 but the indicated horse powers were in the ratio 335 : 281. At equal power *Rattler* would have made 8.7 knots and been beaten by *Alecto.*

Later the same day the two ships followed a 34-mile course using both sail and steam over which *Rattler* made 11.9 knots and *Alecto* 11.2. The following day *Rattler* beat *Alecto* in a strong head wind under steam alone. Three more races using sail alone were all won by *Rattler*. For these, *Alecto* removed her lower paddle boards and *Rattler* set her two-bladed screw vertically in the deadwood.

Nominal hp	Machinery	Builder	No of Cyls	rpm	Propulsor dia.
					ft. ins.
200	Vertical 'Siamese'	Maudslay	4	25	10 1
200	Direct	Seaward and Capel	2	14	21 0

Two most informative trials followed in which each ship in turn was towed by the other. *Rattler* was able to tow *Alecto*, still with paddles removed, at about 7 knots with 352ihp while *Alecto* could tow *Rattler* at only 6 knots.

Then on 3 April 1845 came the famous tug-of-war so often described incorrectly as the event which brought the screw into the Navy. Sportingly, the trial was set up to give the *Alecto* every chance. She was allowed to move off first and was towing *Rattler* astern at 2 knots before the screw started to turn. Five minutes later *Rattler* had arrested her sternway and soon she moved forward pulling *Alecto* backwards, despite her thrashing paddles at 2.8 knots. *Rattler* developed 300ihp while under these conditions *Alecto* could must only 141ihp. Almost certainly this trial was planned as a public relations exercise to convince the remaining doubters.

Rattler alone then ran two trials at reduced power which are useful for analysis. The screw won yet another race and then *Alecto* won for the first time against a strong head wind and heavy seas. *Rattler* had to close her engine room openings and lost steam pressure in consequence. The last trial was abandoned with *Rattler* in the lead when *Alecto* had serious boiler trouble.

The most important data for *Rattler* are:

Speed (Kts)	N (RPM)	ihp	Thrust (tons)
9.2	23.75	335	3.89
8.0	21.0	205	2.76
6.0	17.0	127	2.15

The speed/rpm relationship is linear and gives an advance coefficient of 1.0. Non-dimensional plots of thrust and ihp suggest that the data are reliable and consistent except for the thrust at 6 knots which seems low.

Using propeller data from the AEW (Admiralty Experimental Works, Haslar), 1953 series (3-blade) for BAR = 0.2, pitch 11ft and diameter 10ft (P/D = 1.1) it is possible to deduce a thrust identity wake for the ship.

V (knots)	9.2	8.0	6.0
wake w $\frac{(V-V')}{V}$	0.2	0.17	0.14

These seem credible figures for a rather bluff, single-screw ship.

Using the Taylor-Gertlor series, the resistance of the smooth, clean ship can be deduced.

These figures are plotted on the graph shown, with the measured thrust values.

The difference between the smooth hull resistance and the thrust is due to roughness and thrust deduction and the effects cannot be fully separated. Almost certainly the thrust deduction was over 20 per cent and accounted for *Rattler's* relatively poor results compared with *Alecto* at equal power.

Also shown in the graph is a single spot for the thrust developed by *Rattler* when towing *Alecto*. This is much higher and is made up of the augmented resistance of *Rattler* in the towing condition together with the bare hull resistance of *Alecto* (possibly increased by *Rattler's* propeller race).

However, the hydrodynamics of screw propulsion was really a side issue and was recognised as such at the time. Provided that performance was comparable, the screw ship was a far more effective warship with its unobstructed broadside, submerged propulsor and better sailing characteristics. The fully submerged screw was far less sensitive to pitch and roll and also to changes of draught.

FURTHER TRIALS

Though the Navy was committed to the screw, trials continued. There was no science of model testing so all developments had to be tried on full scale. With no guiding theory, extrapolation of the results to different ships and propellers was difficult and wrong answers not uncommon.

The tender *Dwarf*, purchased in 1843 and probably the first screw ship to enter the RN, was used for a long series of tests in 1845. Some fifteen propellers were tried with variations in pitch and blade area the best giving her 9.1 knots at 32rpm. Lloyd then tried the effect of variations in stern lines. The stern was filled out with three layers of thick planks, carefully faired to give a smooth, if bluff, shape. At full power *Dwarf* could now reach only 3.25 knots at 24rpm. With one layer of planks removed she made 5.75 knots at 26.5rpm and with all planks off the speed was back to 9 knots. During 1847-8, further comparisons between fine and full sterns were made between *Sharpshooter/Rifleman* and *Minx/Teazer*, the first of each pair having the fine stern.

In May and August the *Niger* (screw) was matched against the paddler, *Basilisk*, in trials:

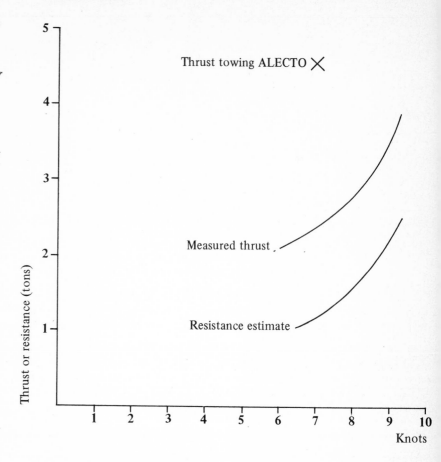

RATTLER

Thrust towing ALECTO ✕

Measured thrust

Resistance estimate

Thrust or resistance (tons)

Knots

1 Under steam alone at three
draughts, including reduced power,
towing trials and a tug-of-war (fig 4).
2 Sail and steam combined at two
draughts.
3 Sail alone at three draughts.

Altogether thirty-three trials were
carried out to little benefit. *Basilisk*
was the more powerful ship and
usually won but at equal power there
was little significant difference. Of
much more significance was the fact
that the top of *Niger's* engine was
4ft 2in below the waterline while that
of *Basilisk* was 6ft 8in above. The
screw engine was 54 tons lighter and
a further 95 tons was saved in the
hull due to the absense of paddle
sponsons and their supports.

There were still more trials to
come, inevitable because the screw
propulsion system was not yet per-
fected. Heavy vibration helped to
cause early failure of the stern gland,
particularly in flexible wooden ships

and as late as 1856 the battleship
Prince Albert nearly foundered from
this cause.

The ultimate end of the competition between screw and paddle came
in the trials of the *Bee,* an instruction-
al vessel for the RN College. She had
both paddles and screw, worked off a
single engine, which could be used in
opposition. The paddles usually won
since the rotational speed was too
low for the screw.

CONCLUSION

The end of the overture came on
23 September 1846 when HMS *Ajax*
went to sea, the world's first seagoing
steam battleship. Lest anyone still
feel that their Lordships were tardy
in introducing the screw, let it be
noted that Samuel Cunard built his
last transatlantic paddler in 1861 and
did not convert her to screw until
1879.

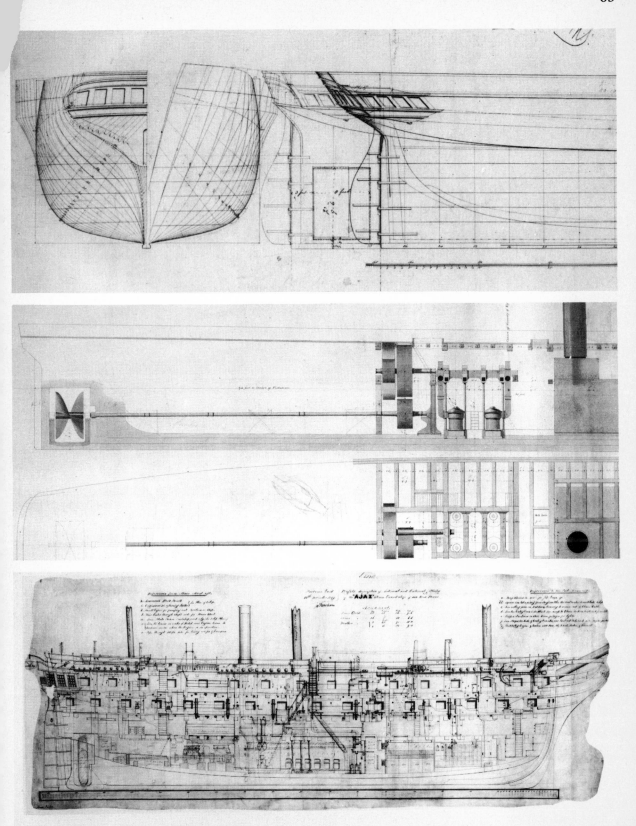

Warship Photograph Service

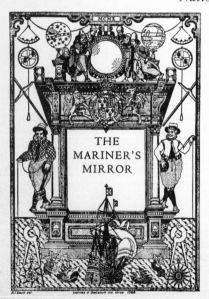